W9-BYA-568

Presented to

James Wm. Fusaro

on

_5 . 27 . 15_

by

mom, Lorenzo,
James, Christopher
& William

When I was young I was sure of everything; in a few years, having been mistaken a thousand times, I was not half so sure of most things as I was before; at present, I am hardly sure of anything but what God has revealed to me.
—JOHN WESLEY

SPIRIT LED PROMISES FOR

GRADS

PASSIO
THE ART OF AUTHENTIC FAITH

MEV

MODERN
ENGLISH
VERSION

Most CHARISMA HOUSE BOOK GROUP products are available at special quantity discounts for bulk purchase for sales promotions, premiums, fund-raising, and educational needs. For details, write Charisma House Book Group, 600 Rinehart Road, Lake Mary, Florida 32746, or telephone (407) 333-0600.

SPIRITLED PROMISES FOR GRADS
Published by Passio
Charisma Media/Charisma House Book Group
600 Rinehart Road
Lake Mary, Florida 32746
www.charismahouse.com

This book or parts thereof may not be reproduced in any form, stored in a retrieval system, or transmitted in any form by any means—electronic, mechanical, photocopy, recording, or otherwise—without prior written permission of the publisher, except as provided by United States of America copyright law.

All Scripture quotations are taken from the Modern English Version. Copyright © 2014 by Military Bible Association. Used by permission. All rights reserved.

Copyright © 2015 by Passio
All rights reserved

Cover design by Lisa Rae McClure
Design Director: Justin Evans

Visit the Passio and Modern English Version websites: www.passiofaith.com and www.mevbible.com.

Library of Congress Control Number: 2014922774
International Standard Book Number: 978-1-62998-225-0
E-book ISBN: 978-1-62998-248-9

First edition

15 16 17 18 19 — 987654321
Printed in the United States of America

*I am confident of this very thing, that
He who began a good work in you will
perfect it until the day of Jesus Christ.*

—Philippians 1:6

CONTENTS

When a train goes through a tunnel
and it gets dark, you don't throw
away the ticket and jump off. You
sit still and trust the engineer.

—CORRIE TEN BOOM

INTRODUCTION

For I know the plans that I have for you, says the LORD,
plans for peace and not for evil, to give you a future
and a hope. Then you shall call upon Me, and you
shall come and pray to Me, and I will listen to you.
—JEREMIAH 29:11–12

D O YOU HAVE a fire burning inside you—a desire to
discover God's purpose for your life? Something you
can be passionate about and, by pursuing it, make a difference in the world? One thing you can rely on: you're here
because God put you here, and He has important work
for you to do.

It's time to discover what's essential for your life. Finding
the one thing that stirs the passion within you is made easier
when you look to God and His word for direction. When
you discover your mission, you will feel its demand. It will
fill you with enthusiasm and a burning desire to make it a
successful calling. Exploring the promises God has made
will provide you with direction, enduring encouragement,
motivation, and perspective as you step out into the real
world and the challenges of the calling before you.

SpiritLed Promises for Grads will nourish and replenish
your heart, mind, and soul. You'll experience your spirit

1

energized from the comforting scriptures of God's Word. These are specially selected promises for two hundred important life topics that renew your strength, hope, comfort, and confidence for everything that life delivers. Apply each scripture personally, and you'll experience the power of God's Word in action. You'll realize the joy in celebrating victories in many areas of your life when you learn to trust God to meet your every need.

Sometimes it can be difficult to live a faith-filled life. When you feel discouraged, remember that God knows what you're going through and is right there with you. Whenever you struggle against God's plans, you suffer. When you resist God's calling, your efforts bear little fruit. The best strategy, therefore, is to seek God's wisdom and to follow Him where He chooses to lead. He wants you to become secure enough in His promises that you can confront fear, take risks, and make the commitments that provide the direction for the paths He has directed for your life.

SpiritLed Promises for Grads reveals the heart of the eternal God, and every promise is personal to you. By spending just a few minutes during the quiet times of your day, you'll find that God still speaks anew through the words of the Bible today—even through verses you've read many times before. Opens your eyes to the truth in a way that frees you from things that pull you down, such as jealousy, anger, hurt, and strife. Allow God's promises to plant seeds of hope within you that help you grow into the person God has destined you to be. As you read, you'll discover how frequently a promise from the Scriptures can offer insight and answers that turn a situation around in an instant. You'll find promises that will help you maintain your faith during times of struggle and direction to help you with navigating life, work, and relationships.

Most of the time, trusting God involves placing a situation in His hands, believing He will either change it or give you what you need to endure it. God is faithful and will never let you down. He is there for you today, tomorrow, and all the days that follow. God has promised to keep you mindful of His words, but for Him to remind you, you need to know what He has said. What are you trusting God for right now? Take whatever it is—no matter how big or how small, possible, or impossible—and place it in God's capable hands. Rely on His promises to see you through to victory.

Refuse to be average. Let your heart soar as high as it will.

—A. W. Tozer

ACCEPTING OTHERS

A man who has friends must show himself friendly, and there is a friend who sticks closer than a brother.

—Proverbs 18:24

He has told you, O man, what is good—and what does the Lord require of you, but to do justice and to love kindness, and to walk humbly with your God?

—Micah 6:8

This is My commandment: that you love one another, as I have loved you. Greater love has no man than this: that a man lay down his life for his friends.

—John 15:12–13

Then Peter began to speak, saying, "Truthfully, I perceive that God is no respecter of persons. But in every nation he who fears Him and works righteousness is accepted by Him."

—Acts 10:34–35

Be devoted to one another with brotherly love; prefer one another in honor.

—Romans 12:10

ACCOUNTABILITY

But I say to you that for every idle word that men speak, they will give an account on the Day of Judgment. For by your words you will be justified, and by your words you will be condemned.

—Matthew 12:36–37

He told His disciples: "There was a rich man who had a steward who was accused to the man of wasting his resources. So he called him and said, 'How is it that I hear this about you? Give an account of your stewardship, for you may no longer be steward.'"

—Luke 16:1–2

So then each of us shall give an account of himself to God.

—Romans 14:12

For we must all appear before the judgment seat of Christ, that each one may receive his recompense in the body, according to what he has done, whether it was good or bad.

—2 Corinthians 5:10

Obey your leaders and submit to them, for they watch over your souls as those who must give an account. Let them do this with joy and not complaining, for that would not be profitable to you.

—Hebrews 13:17

ALCOHOL

Wine is a mocker, strong drink is raging, and whoever is deceived by it is not wise.

—Proverbs 20:1

Do not be among winebibbers, among riotous eaters of meat; for the drunkard and the glutton will come to poverty, and drowsiness will clothe a man with rags.

—Proverbs 23:20–21

I urge you therefore, brothers, by the mercies of God, that you present your bodies as a living sacrifice, holy, and acceptable to God, which is your reasonable service of worship. Do not be conformed to this world, but be transformed by the renewing of your mind, that you may prove what is the good and acceptable and perfect will of God.

—Romans 12:1–2

Do you not know that the unrighteous will not inherit the kingdom of God? Do not be deceived. Neither the sexually immoral, nor idolaters, nor adulterers, nor male prostitutes, nor homosexuals, nor thieves, nor covetous, nor drunkards, nor revilers, nor extortioners will inherit the kingdom of God.

—1 Corinthians 6:9–10

Envy, murders, drunkenness, carousing, and the like. I warn you, as I previously warned you, that those who do such things shall not inherit the kingdom of God.

—Galatians 5:21

ANGER

Do not be quick in your spirit to be angry, for irritation settles in the bosom of fools.

—Ecclesiastes 7:9

But I say to you that whoever is angry with his brother without a cause shall be in danger of the judgment. And whoever says

9

to his brother, "Raca," shall be in danger of the Sanhedrin. But whoever says, "You fool," shall be in danger of hell fire.

—Matthew 5:22

Beloved, do not avenge yourselves, but rather give place to God's wrath, for it is written: "Vengeance is Mine. I will repay," says the Lord. Therefore "If your enemy is hungry, feed him; if he is thirsty, give him a drink; for in doing so you will heap coals of fire on his head." Do not be overcome by evil, but overcome evil with good.

—Romans 12:19–21

Be angry but do not sin. Do not let the sun go down on your anger.

—Ephesians 4:26

Let all bitterness, wrath, anger, outbursts, and blasphemies, with all malice, be taken away from you. And be kind one to another, tenderhearted, forgiving one another, just as God in Christ also forgave you.

—Ephesians 4:31–32

ANOINTING

The Spirit of the Lord is upon Me, because He has anointed Me to preach the gospel to the poor; He has sent Me to heal the broken-hearted, to preach deliverance to the captives and recovery of sight to the blind, to set at liberty those who are oppressed.

—LUKE 4:18

Truly, truly I say to you, he who believes in Me will do the works that I do also. And he will do greater works than these, because I am going to My Father.

—JOHN 14:12

But the fruit of the Spirit is love, joy, peace, patience, gentleness, goodness, faith, meekness, and self-control; against such there is no law.

—GALATIANS 5:22–23

But you have an anointing from the Holy One, and you know all things. I have written to you, not because you do not know the truth, but because you know it, and because no lie is of the truth. Who is a liar but the one who denies that Jesus is the Christ? Whoever denies the Father and the Son is the antichrist.

—1 JOHN 2:20–22

But the anointing which you have received from Him remains in you, and you do not need anyone to teach you. For as the same anointing teaches you concerning all things, and is truth, and is no lie, and just as it has taught you, remain in Him.

—1 JOHN 2:27

ANSWERED PRAYER

Call to Me, and I will answer you, and show you great and mighty things which you do not know.

—Jeremiah 33:3

Ask and it will be given to you; seek and you will find; knock and it will be opened to you.

—Matthew 7:7

Therefore I say to you, whatever things you ask when you pray, believe that you will receive them, and you will have them.

—Mark 11:24

If you remain in Me, and My words remain in you, you will ask whatever you desire, and it shall be done for you.

—John 15:7

Confess your faults to one another and pray for one another, that you may be healed. The effective, fervent prayer of a righteous man accomplishes much.

—James 5:16

ANXIETY

God is able to make all grace abound toward you, so that you, always having enough of everything, may abound to every good work.

—2 Corinthians 9:8

For God has not given us the spirit of fear, but of power, and love, and self-control.

—2 Timothy 1:7

Let your lives be without love of money, and be content with the things you have. For He has said: "I will never leave you, nor forsake you."

—Hebrews 13:5

So we may boldly say, "The Lord is my helper, I will not fear. What can man do to me?"

—Hebrews 13:6

Let us then come with confidence to the throne of grace, that we may obtain mercy and find grace to help in time of need.

—Hebrews 4:16

APPEARANCE

Do not judge according to appearance, but practice righteous judgment.

—John 7:24

For we are not commending ourselves again to you. Instead, we give you occasion to boast on our behalf, that you may have something to answer those who boast in appearance and not in heart.

—2 Corinthians 5:12

But of these who seemed to be something—whatever they were, it makes no difference to me; God shows no partiality to anyone—for those who seemed to be something added nothing to me.

—Galatians 2:6

Abstain from all appearances of evil.

—1 Thessalonians 5:22

Do not let your adorning be the outward adorning of braiding the hair, wearing gold, or putting on fine clothing. But let it be the hidden nature of the heart, that which is not corruptible, even the ornament of a gentle and quiet spirit, which is very precious in the sight of God.

—1 Peter 3:3–4

ASSURANCE

For I am persuaded that neither death nor life, neither angels nor principalities nor powers, neither things present nor things to come, neither height nor depth, nor any other created thing, shall be able to separate us from the love of God, which is in Christ Jesus our Lord.

—Romans 8:38–39

God is able to make all grace abound toward you, so that you, always having enough of everything, may abound to every good work.

—2 Corinthians 9:8

According to the eternal purpose which He completed in Christ Jesus our Lord, in whom we have boldness and confident access through faith in Him.

—Ephesians 3:11–12

For these things I suffer, but I am not ashamed, for I know whom I have believed, and am persuaded that He is able to keep that which I have committed to Him until that Day.

—2 Timothy 1:12

Let us draw near with a true heart in full assurance of faith, having our hearts sprinkled to cleanse them from an evil conscience, and our bodies washed with pure water.

—Hebrews 10:22

ATTITUDE

That you put off the former way of life in the old nature, which is corrupt according to the deceitful lusts, and be renewed in the spirit of your mind; and that you put on the new nature, which was created according to God in righteousness and true holiness.

—Ephesians 4:22–24

Let the peace of God, to which also you are called in one body, rule in your hearts. And be thankful.

—Colossians 3:15

Do all things without murmuring and disputing, that you may be blameless and harmless, sons of God, without fault, in

15

the midst of a crooked and perverse generation, in which you shine as lights in the world.

—Philippians 2:14–15

Finally, brothers, whatever things are true, whatever things are honest, whatever things are just, whatever things are pure, whatever things are lovely, whatever things are of good report, if there is any virtue, and if there is any praise, think on these things. Do those things which you have both learned and received, and heard and seen in me, and the God of peace will be with you.

—Philippians 4:8–9

Humble yourselves in the sight of the Lord, and He will lift you up.

—James 4:10

BACKSLIDING

The backslider in heart will be filled with his own ways, but a good man will be satisfied with his.

—Proverbs 14:14

Go and proclaim these words toward the north, and say: Return, backsliding Israel, says the Lord, and I will not cause My anger to fall on you. For I am merciful, says the Lord, and I will not keep anger forever. Only acknowledge your iniquity, that you have transgressed against the Lord your God and have scattered your ways to the strangers under every green tree, and you have not obeyed My voice, says the LORD. Return, O backsliding sons, says the LORD. For I am married to you. And I will take you, one from a city and two from a family, and I will bring you to Zion.

—JEREMIAH 3:12–14

I will give them a heart to know Me, that I am the LORD; and they will be My people, and I will be their God, for they will return to Me with their whole heart.

—JEREMIAH 24:7

Nor shall they defile themselves anymore with their idols, nor with their detestable things, nor with any of their transgressions. But I will save them out of all their dwelling places in which they have sinned and will cleanse them. So they shall be My people, and I will be their God.

—EZEKIEL 37:23

I am the vine, you are the branches. He who remains in Me, and I in him, bears much fruit. For without Me you can do nothing.

—JOHN 15:5

But I have something against you, that you have abandoned the love you had at first. Remember therefore from where you have fallen. Repent, and do the works you did at first, or else I will come to you quickly and remove your candlestick from its place, unless you repent.

—REVELATION 2:4–5

BAD HABITS

The truthful lip will be established forever, but a lying tongue is but for a moment. Deceit is in the heart of those who imagine evil, but to the counselors of peace is joy.

—Proverbs 12:19–20

Lying lips are abomination to the Lord, but those who deal truly are His delight.

—Proverbs 12:22

He who has a deceitful heart finds no good, and he who has a perverse tongue falls into mischief.

—Proverbs 17:20

But avoid profane foolish babblings, for they will increase to more ungodliness.

—2 Timothy 2:16

Therefore submit yourselves to God. Resist the devil, and he will flee from you.

—James 4:7

Live your lives honorably among the Gentiles, so that though they speak against you as evildoers, they shall see your good works and thereby glorify God in the day of visitation.

—1 Peter 2:12

BATTLE FOR YOUR MIND

You will keep him in perfect peace, whose mind is stayed on You, because he trusts in You.

—Isaiah 26:3

Then Jesus said to those Jews who believed Him, "If you remain in My word, then you are truly My disciples. You shall know the truth, and the truth shall set you free."

—John 8:31–32

For the weapons of our warfare are not carnal, but mighty through God to the pulling down of strongholds, casting down imaginations and every high thing that exalts itself against the knowledge of God, bringing every thought into captivity to the obedience of Christ.

—2 Corinthians 10:4–5

Therefore this I say and testify in the Lord, that from now on you walk not as other Gentiles walk, in the vanity of their minds.

—Ephesians 4:17

Little children, let no one deceive you. The one who does righteousness is righteous, just as Christ is righteous.

—1 John 3:7

BEAUTY

Who can find a virtuous woman? For her worth is far above rubies.

—Proverbs 31:10

Strength and honor are her clothing, and she will rejoice in time to come. She opens her mouth with wisdom, and in her tongue is the teaching of kindness.

—Proverbs 31:25–26

Charm is deceitful, and beauty is vain, but a woman who fears the Lord, she shall be praised.

—Proverbs 31:30

He has made everything beautiful in its appropriate time. He has also put obscurity in their hearts so that no one comes to know the work that God has done from the beginning to the end.

—Ecclesiastes 3:11

Finally, brothers, whatever things are true, whatever things are honest, whatever things are just, whatever things are pure, whatever things are lovely, whatever things are of good report, if there is any virtue, and if there is any praise, think on these things.

—Philippians 4:8

BITTERNESS

Bless those who persecute you; bless, and do not curse.

—ROMANS 12:14

Repay no one evil for evil. Commend what is honest in the sight of all men.

—ROMANS 12:17

Pursue peace with all men, and the holiness without which no one will see the Lord, watching diligently so that no one falls short of the grace of God, lest any root of bitterness spring up to cause trouble, and many become defiled by it.

—HEBREWS 12:14–15

Out of the same mouth proceed blessing and cursing. My brothers, these things ought not to be so.

—JAMES 3:10

For to this you were called, because Christ suffered for us, leaving us an example, that you should follow His steps. "He committed no sin, nor was deceit found in His mouth."

—1 PETER 2:21–22

BLAME

Judge not, that you be not judged. For with what judgment you judge, you will be judged. And with the measure you use, it will be measured again for you. And why do you see the speck that is in your brother's eye, but do not consider the plank that is in your own eye? Or how will you say to your brother, "Let me pull the speck out of your eye," when a log is in your own eye? You hypocrite! First take the plank out of your own eye, and then you will see clearly to take the speck out of your brother's eye.

—Matthew 7:1–5

I have told you these things so that in Me you may have peace. In the world you will have tribulation. But be of good cheer. I have overcome the world.

—John 16:33

Not only so, but we also boast in tribulation, knowing that tribulation produces patience, patience produces character, and character produces hope. And hope does not disappoint, because the love of God is shed abroad in our hearts by the Holy Spirit who has been given to us.

—Romans 5:3–5

My brothers, count it all joy when you fall into diverse temptations, knowing that the trying of your faith develops patience. But let patience perfect its work, that you may be perfect and complete, lacking nothing.

—James 1:2–4

Blessed is the man who endures temptation, for when he is tried, he will receive the crown of life, which the Lord has promised to those who love Him.

—James 1:12

BLESSINGS

Then Jabez called on the God of Israel, saying, "Oh, that You would indeed bless me and enlarge my territory, that Your hand might be with me, and that You would keep me from evil, that it may not bring me hardship!" So God granted what he asked.

—1 Chronicles 4:10

For I, the Lord your God, will hold your right hand, saying to you, "Do not fear; I will help you."

—Isaiah 41:13

The Lord has been mindful of us; He will bless us; He will bless the house of Israel; He will bless the house of Aaron. He will bless those who fear the Lord, both the small and great ones. The Lord shall increase you more and more, you and your children.

—Psalm 115:12–14

Give, and it will be given to you: Good measure, pressed down, shaken together, and running over will men give unto you. For with the measure you use, it will be measured unto you.

—Luke 6:38

BREAKTHROUGH

Surely He shall deliver you from the snare of the hunter and from the deadly pestilence. He shall cover you with His feathers, and under His wings you shall find protection; His faithfulness shall be your shield and wall. You shall not be afraid of the terror by night, nor of the arrow that flies by day.

—Psalm 91:3–5

No weapon that is formed against you shall prosper, and every tongue that shall rise against you in judgment, you shall condemn. This is the heritage of the servants of the Lord, and their vindication is from Me, says the Lord.

—Isaiah 54:17

Then your light shall break forth as the morning, and your healing shall spring forth quickly, and your righteousness shall go before you; the glory of the Lord shall be your reward.

—Isaiah 58:8

Or else how can one enter a strong man's house and plunder his goods unless he first binds the strong man? And then he will plunder his house.

—Matthew 12:29

You are of God, little children, and have overcome them, because He who is in you is greater than he who is in the world.

—1 John 4:4

BROKENNESS

The righteous cry out, and the Lord hears, and delivers them out of all their troubles. The Lord is near to the brokenhearted, and saves the contrite of spirit. Many are the afflictions of the righteous, but the Lord delivers him out of them all. A righteous one keeps all his bones; not one of them is broken.

—Psalm 34:17–20

He has put a new song in my mouth, even praise to our God; many will see it, and fear, and will trust in the Lord.

—Psalm 40:3

I will praise the name of God with a song, and will magnify Him with thanksgiving.

—Psalm 69:30

He heals the broken in heart, and binds up their wounds.

—Psalm 147:3

Moreover the light of the moon shall be as the light of the sun, and the light of the sun shall be sevenfold, as the light of seven days, in the day that the Lord binds up the breach of His people and heals the wound from His blow.

—Isaiah 30:26

No temptation has taken you except what is common to man. God is faithful, and He will not permit you to be tempted above what you can endure, but will with the temptation also make a way to escape, that you may be able to bear it.

—1 Corinthians 10:13

BURNOUT

See, the LORD your God has set the land before you. Go up and possess it, just as the LORD, the God of your fathers, spoke to you. Do not fear or be discouraged.

—DEUTERONOMY 1:21

But those who wait upon the LORD shall renew their strength; they shall mount up with wings as eagles, they shall run and not be weary, and they shall walk and not faint.

—ISAIAH 40:31

Do not fear, for I am with you; do not be dismayed, for I am your God. I will strengthen you, I will help you, yes, I will uphold you with My righteous right hand.

—ISAIAH 41:10

Return to your stronghold, prisoners who now have hope. Today I declare that I will return to you a double portion.

—ZECHARIAH 9:12

And let us not grow weary in doing good, for in due season we shall reap, if we do not give up.

—GALATIANS 6:9

"God shall wipe away all tears from their eyes. There shall be no more death." Neither shall there be any more sorrow nor crying nor pain, for the former things have passed away.

—REVELATION 21:4

BUSINESS

But you must remember the Lord your God, for it is He who gives you the ability to get wealth, so that He may establish His covenant which He swore to your fathers, as it is today.

—Deuteronomy 8:18

My son, attend to my words; incline your ear to my sayings. Do not let them depart from your eyes; keep them in the midst of your heart; for they are life to those who find them, and health to all their body.

—Proverbs 4:20–22

Whatever your hands find to do, do with your strength; for there is no work or planning or knowledge or wisdom in Sheol, the place where you are going.

—Ecclesiastes 9:10

And the Lord answered me: Write the vision, and make it plain on tablets, that he who reads it may run.

—Habakkuk 2:2

No one can serve two masters. For either he will hate the one and love the other, or else he will hold to the one and despise the other. You cannot serve God and money.

—Matthew 6:24

And whatever you do in word or deed, do all in the name of the Lord Jesus, giving thanks to God the Father through Him.

—Colossians 3:17

CHALLENGES

No man will be able to stand against you all the days of your life. As I was with Moses, I will be with you. I will not abandon you. I will not leave you.

—Joshua 1:5

When I was a child, I spoke as a child, I understood as a child, and I thought as a child. But when I became a man, I put away childish things.

—1 Corinthians 13:11

We are troubled on every side, yet not distressed; we are perplexed, but not in despair; persecuted, but not forsaken; cast down, but not destroyed.

—2 Corinthians 4:8–9

I can do all things because of Christ who strengthens me.

—Philippians 4:13

My brothers, count it all joy when you fall into diverse temptations, knowing that the trying of your faith develops patience. But let patience perfect its work, that you may be perfect and complete, lacking nothing.

—James 1:2–4

CHANGE

Be strong and of a good courage. Fear not, nor be afraid of them, for the Lord your God, it is He who goes with you. He will not fail you, nor forsake you.

—Deuteronomy 31:6

My son, do not forget my teaching, but let your heart keep my commandments; for length of days and long life and peace will they add to you.

—Proverbs 3:1–2

I urge you therefore, brothers, by the mercies of God, that you present your bodies as a living sacrifice, holy, and acceptable to God, which is your reasonable service of worship. Do not be conformed to this world, but be transformed by the renewing of your mind, that you may prove what is the good and acceptable and perfect will of God.

—Romans 12:1–2

Listen, I tell you a mystery: We shall not all sleep, but we shall all be changed.

—1 Corinthians 15:51

Every good gift and every perfect gift is from above and comes down from the Father of lights, with whom is no change or shadow of turning.

—James 1:17

CHARACTER

And you shall love the Lord your God with all your heart and with all your soul and with all your might. These words, which I am commanding you today, shall be in your heart.

—Deuteronomy 6:5–6

Trust in the Lord with all your heart, and lean not on your own understanding; in all your ways acknowledge Him, and He will direct your paths. Do not be wise in your own eyes; fear the Lord and depart from evil. It will be health to your body, and strength to your bones.

—Proverbs 3:5–8

A good name is rather to be chosen than great riches, and loving favor rather than silver and gold. The rich and poor have this in common, the Lord is the maker of them all.

—Proverbs 22:1–2

For to the person who is pleasing before Him, God gives wisdom, knowledge, and joy; but to the sinner He gives the work of gathering and collecting to give him who is pleasing before God. Also this is vanity and chasing the wind.

—Ecclesiastes 2:26

Likewise you younger ones, submit yourselves to the elders. Yes, all of you be submissive one to another and clothe yourselves with humility, because "God resists the proud, but gives grace to the humble."

—1 Peter 5:5

CHEATING

He who walks uprightly walks surely, but he who perverts his ways will be known.

—Proverbs 10:9

Lying lips are abomination to the Lord, but those who deal truly are His delight.

—Proverbs 12:22

Better is the poor who walks in his integrity, than he who is perverse in his lips and is a fool.

—Proverbs 19:1

He who is faithful in what is least is faithful also in much. And he who is dishonest in the least is dishonest also in much. So if you have not been faithful in the unrighteous wealth, who will commit to your trust the true riches? And if you have not been faithful in that which is another man's, who will give you that which is your own?

—Luke 16:10–12

Be not deceived. God is not mocked. For whatever a man sows, that will he also reap. For the one who sows to his own flesh will from the flesh reap corruption, but the one who sows to the Spirit will from the Spirit reap eternal life.

—Galatians 6:7–8

CHRISTLIKENESS

For those whom He foreknew, He predestined to be conformed to the image of His Son, so that He might be the firstborn among many brothers.

—Romans 8:29

But we all, seeing the glory of the Lord with unveiled faces, as in a mirror, are being transformed into the same image from glory to glory by the Spirit of the Lord.

—2 Corinthians 3:18

But, speaking the truth in love, we may grow up in all things into Him, who is the head, Christ Himself.

—Ephesians 4:15

Therefore, my beloved, as you have always obeyed, not only in my presence, but so much more in my absence, work out your own salvation with fear and trembling. For God is the One working in you, both to will and to do His good pleasure.

—Philippians 2:12–13

But grow in the grace and knowledge of our Lord and Savior Jesus Christ. To Him be glory, both now and forever. Amen.

—2 Peter 3:18

COMMITMENT

See, I am setting before you today a blessing and a curse: the blessing if you obey the commandments of the LORD your God, which I am commanding you today, and the curse, if you will not obey the commandments of the LORD your God, but turn from the way which I am commanding you today, to go after other gods which you have not known.

—DEUTERONOMY 11:26–28

And I will give them one heart and one way, that they may fear Me forever, for their good and for their children after them. And I will make an everlasting covenant with them that I will not turn away from them, to do them good. But I will put My fear in their hearts so that they shall not depart from Me.

—JEREMIAH 32:39–40

Whoever will confess Me before men, him will I confess also before My Father who is in heaven. But whoever will deny Me before men, him will I also deny before My Father who is in heaven.

—MATTHEW 10:32–33

If a man does not remain in Me, he is thrown out as a branch and withers. And they gather them and throw them into the fire, and they are burned. If you remain in Me, and My words remain in you, you will ask whatever you desire, and it shall be done for you.

—JOHN 15:6–7

For I am persuaded that neither death nor life, neither angels nor principalities nor powers, neither things present nor things to come, neither height nor depth, nor any other created thing, shall be able to separate us from the love of God, which is in Christ Jesus our Lord.

—Romans 8:38–39

COMPETITION

Do you not know that all those who run in a race run, but one receives the prize? So run, that you may obtain it.

—1 Corinthians 9:24

Let nothing be done out of strife or conceit, but in humility let each esteem the other better than himself. Let each of you look not only to your own interests, but also to the interests of others.

—Philippians 2:3–4

I can do all things because of Christ who strengthens me.

—Philippians 4:13

And whatever you do, do it heartily, as for the Lord and not for men.

—Colossians 3:23

Anyone who competes as an athlete is not rewarded without competing legally.

—2 Timothy 2:5

But He gives more grace. For this reason it says: "God resists the proud, but gives grace to the humble."

—James 4:6

COMPLAINING

Let no unwholesome word proceed out of your mouth, but only that which is good for building up, that it may give grace to the listeners.

—Ephesians 4:29

Do all things without murmuring and disputing.

—Philippians 2:14

In everything give thanks, for this is the will of God in Christ Jesus concerning you.

—1 Thessalonians 5:18

Do not grumble against one another, brothers, lest you be condemned. Look, the Judge is standing at the door.

—James 5:9

Show hospitality to one another without complaining. As everyone has received a gift, even so serve one another with it, as good stewards of the manifold grace of God.

—1 Peter 4:9–10

COMPROMISE

He answered, "'You shall love the Lord your God with all your heart, and with all your soul, and with all your strength, and with all your mind' and 'your neighbor as yourself.'"

—Luke 10:27

If you love Me, keep My commandments.

—John 14:15

Welcome him who is weak in faith, but not for the purpose of arguing over opinions. For one has faith to eat all things, but he who is weak eats only vegetables. Do not let him who eats despise him who does not eat, and do not let him who does not eat judge him who eats, for God has welcomed him. Who are you to judge another man's servant? To his own master he stands or falls. And he will stand, for God is able to make him stand.

—Romans 14:1–4

Do not be unequally yoked together with unbelievers. For what fellowship has righteousness with unrighteousness? What communion has light with darkness? What agreement has Christ with Belial? Or what part has he who believes with an unbeliever? What agreement has the temple of God with idols? For you are the temple of the living God. As God has said: "I will live in them and walk in them. I will be their God, and they shall be My people."

—2 Corinthians 6:14–17

For if we willfully continue to sin after we have received the knowledge of the truth, there no longer remains a sacrifice for sins.

—Hebrews 10:26

Therefore, to him who knows to do good and does not do it, it is sin.

—James 4:17

CONCEIT

For wisdom is better than rubies, and all the things that may be desired are not to be compared to it. I, wisdom, dwell with prudence, and find out knowledge and discretion.

—Proverbs 8:11–12

Pride goes before destruction, and a haughty spirit before a fall. Better it is to be of a humble spirit with the lowly than to divide the spoil with the proud.

—Proverbs 16:18–19

Do you see a man wise in his own conceit? There is more hope for a fool than for him.

—Proverbs 26:12

See, the Lord, the Lord of Hosts, shall lop the bough with terror; and the tall ones of stature shall be hewn down, and the haughty shall be humbled.

—Isaiah 10:33

Be of the same mind toward one another. Do not be haughty, but associate with the lowly. Do not pretend to be wiser than you are.

—Romans 12:16

CONDEMNATION

For all have sinned and come short of the glory of God.

—Romans 3:23

There is therefore now no condemnation for those who are in Christ Jesus, who walk not according to the flesh, but according to the Spirit. For the law of the Spirit of life in Christ Jesus has set me free from the law of sin and death.

—Romans 8:1–2

Who is he who condemns? It is Christ who died, yes, who is risen, who is also at the right hand of God, who also intercedes for us.

—Romans 8:34

If I speak with the tongues of men and of angels, and have not love, I have become as sounding brass or a clanging cymbal.

—1 Corinthians 13:1

If we confess our sins, He is faithful and just to forgive us our sins and cleanse us from all unrighteousness.

—1 John 1:9

CONFESSION

I acknowledged my sin to You, and my iniquity I did not conceal. I said, "I will confess my transgressions to the LORD," and You forgave the iniquity of my sin. Selah.

—PSALM 32:5

He who covers his sins will not prosper, but whoever confesses and forsakes them will have mercy.

—PROVERBS 28:13

Whoever will confess Me before men, him will I confess also before My Father who is in heaven. But whoever will deny Me before men, him will I also deny before My Father who is in heaven.

—MATTHEW 10:32–33

I say to you, whoever confesses Me before men, him will the Son of Man also confess before the angels of God.

—LUKE 12:8

That if you confess with your mouth Jesus is Lord, and believe in your heart that God has raised Him from the dead, you will be saved, for with the heart one believes unto righteousness, and with the mouth confession is made unto salvation.

—ROMANS 10:9–10

CONFLICT

The beginning of strife is as when one lets out water; therefore abandon contention before a quarrel starts.

—Proverbs 17:14

The discretion of a man defers his anger, and it is his glory to pass over a transgression.

—Proverbs 19:11

Make no friendship with an angry man, and with a furious man you will not go, lest you learn his ways and get a snare to your soul.

—Proverbs 22:24–25

Blessed are the peacemakers, for they shall be called the sons of God.

—Matthew 5:9

But I say to you, love your enemies, bless those who curse you, do good to those who hate you, and pray for those who spitefully use you and persecute you.

—Matthew 5:44

CONSEQUENCES

But your iniquities have made a separation between you and your God, and your sins have hidden His face from you so that He will not hear.

—Isaiah 59:2

The heart is more deceitful than all things and desperately wicked; who can understand it? I, the Lord, search the heart, I test the mind, even to give to every man according to his ways, and according to the fruit of his deeds.

—Jeremiah 17:9–10

Rulers are not a terror to good works, but to evil works. Do you wish to have no fear of the authority? Do what is good, and you will have praise from him, for he is the servant of God for your good.

—Romans 13:3–4

Be not deceived. God is not mocked. For whatever a man sows, that will he also reap. For the one who sows to his own flesh will from the flesh reap corruption, but the one who sows to the Spirit will from the Spirit reap eternal life.

—Galatians 6:7–8

For whoever shall keep the whole law and yet offend in one point is guilty of breaking the whole law.

—James 2:10

CONTENTMENT

The backslider in heart will be filled with his own ways, but a good man will be satisfied with his.

—Proverbs 14:14

Better is a little with righteousness than great revenues with injustice.

—Proverbs 16:8

I experienced that there is nothing better for them than to be glad and do good in their life. And also that everyone should eat and drink and experience good in all their labor. This is a gift of God.

—Ecclesiastes 3:12–13

I do not speak because I have need, for I have learned in whatever state I am to be content. I know both how to face humble circumstances and how to have abundance. Everywhere and in all things I have learned the secret, both to be full and to be hungry, both to abound and to suffer need. I can do all things because of Christ who strengthens me.

—Philippians 4:11–13

But godliness with contentment is great gain.

—1 Timothy 6:6

COURAGE

Have not I commanded you? Be strong and courageous. Do not be afraid or dismayed, for the Lord your God is with you wherever you go.

—Joshua 1:9

Be strong and let us fight with resolve for the sake of our people and the cities of our God. May the Lord do what seems good to Him.

—2 Samuel 10:12

Then you will prosper if you carefully observe the statutes and the judgments which the Lord commanded Moses for Israel. Be strong and of good courage. Do not be afraid or dismayed.

—1 Chronicles 22:13

Trust in the Lord, and do good; dwell in the land, and practice faithfulness.

—Psalm 37:3

He gives power to the faint, and to those who have no might He increases strength.

—Isaiah 40:29

CREATIVITY

We have diverse gifts according to the grace that is given to us: if prophecy, according to the proportion of faith; If service, in serving; he who teaches, in teaching; He who exhorts, in exhortation; he who gives, with generosity; he who rules, with diligence; he who shows mercy, with cheerfulness.

—Romans 12:6–8

By Him you are enriched in everything, in all speech and in all knowledge.

—1 Corinthians 1:5

For I would that all men were even as I myself. But every man has his proper gift from God, one after this manner and another after that.

—1 Corinthians 7:7

There are various gifts, but the same Spirit. There are differences of administrations, but the same Lord. There are various operations, but it is the same God who operates all of them in all people.

—1 Corinthians 12:4–6

Every good gift and every perfect gift is from above and comes down from the Father of lights, with whom is no change or shadow of turning.

—James 1:17

CRISIS

The righteous cry out, and the Lord hears, and delivers them out of all their troubles. The Lord is near to the brokenhearted, and saves the contrite of spirit. Many are the afflictions of the righteous, but the Lord delivers him out of them all. A righteous one keeps all his bones; not one of them is broken.

—Psalm 34:17–20

But he who endures to the end shall be saved.

—Matthew 24:13

Therefore watch always and pray that you may be counted worthy to escape all these things that will happen and to stand before the Son of Man.

—Luke 21:36

But He said to me, "My grace is sufficient for you, for My strength is made perfect in weakness." Therefore most gladly I will boast in my weaknesses, that the power of Christ may rest upon me.

—2 Corinthians 12:9

But my God shall supply your every need according to His riches in glory by Christ Jesus.

Philippians 4:19

CRITICISM

O Lord my God, in You I put my trust; save me from all those who persecute me, and deliver me.

—Psalm 7:1

When pride comes, then comes shame; but with the humble is wisdom.

—Proverbs 11:2

Blessed are you when men revile you, and persecute you, and say all kinds of evil against you falsely for My sake.

—Matthew 5:11

You have heard that it was said, "You shall love your neighbor and hate your enemy." But I say to you, love your enemies, bless those who curse you, do good to those who hate you, and pray for those who spitefully use you and persecute you.

—Matthew 5:43–44

Remember the word that I said to you: "A servant is not greater than his master." If they persecuted Me, they will also persecute you. If they kept My words, they will keep yours also.

—John 15:20

DATING

How shall a young man keep his way pure? By keeping it according to Your word.

—Psalm 119:9

Do not be deceived: "Bad company corrupts good morals."

—1 Corinthians 15:33

Do not be unequally yoked together with unbelievers. For what fellowship has righteousness with unrighteousness? What communion has light with darkness?

—2 Corinthians 6:14

Walk in love, as Christ loved us and gave Himself for us as a fragrant offering and a sacrifice to God. And do not let sexual immorality, or any impurity, or greed be named among you, as these are not proper among saints.

—Ephesians 5:2–3

So flee youthful desires and pursue righteousness, faith, love, and peace, with those who call on the Lord out of a pure heart.

—2 Timothy 2:22

DECEIT

The words of their mouth are wickedness and deceit; they have ceased to be wise and to do good.

—Psalm 36:3

He who practices deceit shall not dwell within my house; he who tells lies shall not remain in my sight.

—Psalm 101:7

Faithful are the wounds of a friend, but the kisses of an enemy are deceitful.

—Proverbs 27:6

Charm is deceitful, and beauty is vain, but a woman who fears the Lord, she shall be praised.

—Proverbs 31:30

The heart is more deceitful than all things and desperately wicked; who can understand it? I, the Lord, search the heart, I test the mind, even to give to every man according to his ways, and according to the fruit of his deeds.

—Jeremiah 17:9–10

DELIVERANCE

He said: The Lord is my rock and my fortress and my deliverer.

—2 Samuel 22:2

For You will cause my lamp to shine; the Lord my God will enlighten my darkness. For by You I can run through a troop, and by my God I can leap a wall.

—Psalm 18:28–29

Many are the afflictions of the righteous, but the Lord delivers him out of them all. A righteous one keeps all his bones; not one of them is broken. Evil will slay the wicked, and those who hate the righteous will be condemned. The Lord redeems the life of His servants, and all who take refuge in Him will not be punished.

—Psalm 34:19–22

But the mercy of the Lord is from everlasting to everlasting upon those who fear Him, and His righteousness to children's children, to those who keep His covenant, and to those who remember to do His commandments.

—Psalm 103:17–18

Awake, awake! Put on your strength, O Zion; put on your beautiful garments, O Jerusalem, the holy city. For the uncircumcised and the unclean will no longer enter you. Shake yourself from the dust; arise, O captive Jerusalem. Loose yourself from the bonds of your neck, O captive daughter of Zion.

—Isaiah 52:1–2

DENIAL

Now it will be, if you will diligently obey the voice of the Lord your God, being careful to do all His commandments which I am commanding you today, then the Lord your God will set you high above all the nations of the earth.

—Deuteronomy 28:1

Whoever, therefore, breaks one of the least of these commandments and teaches others to do likewise shall be called the least in the kingdom of heaven. But whoever does and teaches them shall be called great in the kingdom of heaven.

—Matthew 5:19

But whoever will deny Me before men, him will I also deny before My Father who is in heaven.

—Matthew 10:33

Then He said to them all, "If anyone will come after Me, let him deny himself, and take up his cross daily, and follow Me."

—Luke 9:23

For I am persuaded that neither death nor life, neither angels nor principalities nor powers, neither things present nor things to come, neither height nor depth, nor any other created thing, shall be able to separate us from the love of God, which is in Christ Jesus our Lord.

—Romans 8:38–39

DEPRESSION

Many are the afflictions of the righteous, but the Lord delivers him out of them all.

—Psalm 34:19

The steps of a man are made firm by the Lord; He delights in his way. Though he falls, he will not be hurled down, for the Lord supports him with His hand.

—Psalm 37:23–24

God is our refuge and strength, a well-proven help in trouble. Therefore we will not fear, though the earth be removed, and though the mountains be carried into the midst of the sea; Though its waters roar and foam, though the mountains shake with its swelling. Selah

—Psalm 46:1–3

Create in me a clean heart, O God, and renew a right spirit within me. Do not cast me away from Your presence, and do not take Your Holy Spirit from me. Restore to me the joy of Your salvation, and uphold me with Your willing spirit.

—Psalm 51:10–12

Cast your burden on the Lord, and He will sustain you; He will never allow the righteous to be moved.

—Psalm 55:22

DISAPPOINTMENT

Those who know Your name will put their trust in You, for You, Lord, have not forsaken those who seek You.

—Psalm 9:10

You are my hiding place; You will preserve me from trouble; You will surround me with shouts of deliverance. Selah

—Psalm 32:7

Trust in Him at all times; you people, pour out your heart before Him; God is a shelter for us. Selah

—Psalm 62:8

Blessed are those who mourn, for they shall be comforted.

—Matthew 5:4

Blessed are you poor, for yours is the kingdom of God. Blessed are you who hunger now, for you shall be filled. Blessed are you who weep now, for you shall laugh.

—Luke 6:20–21

DISCIPLESHIP

He who walks righteously and speaks uprightly, he who rejects unjust gain and shakes his hands from holding bribes, who stops his ears from hearing of bloodshed, and shuts his eyes from seeing evil: He shall dwell on high; his place of defense shall be the impregnable rock; his bread shall be given him, his waters shall be sure.

—Isaiah 33:15–16

By this all men will know that you are My disciples, if you have love for one another.

—John 13:35

Jesus answered him, "If a man loves Me, he will keep My word. My Father will love him, and We will come to him, and make Our home with him."

—John 14:23

For those who live according to the flesh set their minds on the things of the flesh, but those who live according to the Spirit, the things of the Spirit.

—Romans 8:5

I have been crucified with Christ. It is no longer I who live, but Christ who lives in me. And the life I now live in the flesh, I live by faith in the Son of God, who loved me and gave Himself for me.

—Galatians 2:20

DISCOURAGEMENT

The sacrifices of God are a broken spirit; a broken and a contrite heart, O God, You will not despise.

—Psalm 51:17

I cried out to God with my voice, even to God with my voice; and He listened to me.

—Psalm 77:1

He heals the broken in heart, and binds up their wounds.

—Psalm 147:3

A merry heart does good like a medicine, but a broken spirit dries the bones.

—Proverbs 17:22

But those who wait upon the Lord shall renew their strength; they shall mount up with wings as eagles, they shall run and not be weary, and they shall walk and not faint.

—Isaiah 40:31

DISTRESS

He lifted up His eyes on His disciples, and said: "Blessed are you poor, for yours is the kingdom of God. Blessed are you who hunger now, for you shall be filled. Blessed are you who weep now, for you shall laugh."

—Luke 6:20–21

Take heed to yourselves, lest your hearts become burdened by excessiveness and drunkenness and anxieties of life, and that Day comes on you unexpectedly. For as a snare it will come on all those who dwell on the face of the whole earth. Therefore watch always and pray that you may be counted worthy to escape all these things that will happen and to stand before the Son of Man.

—Luke 21:34–36

Do not work for the food which perishes, but for that food which endures to eternal life, which the Son of Man will give you. For God the Father has set His seal on Him.

—John 6:27

Listen, my beloved brothers. Has God not chosen the poor of this world to be rich in faith and heirs of the kingdom which He has promised to those who love Him?

—James 2:5

But rejoice insofar as you share in Christ's sufferings, so that you may rejoice and be glad also in the revelation of His glory.

—1 Peter 4:13

DOUBT

The fool has said in his heart, "There is no God." They are corrupt, they do abominable deeds, there is none who does good.

—Psalm 14:1

I will instruct you and teach you in the way you should go; I will counsel you with my eye on you.

—Psalm 32:8

Forever, O Lord, Your word is established in heaven. Your faithfulness is for all generations; You have established the earth, and it is firm.

—Psalm 119:89–90

Trust in the Lord with all your heart, and lean not on your own understanding; in all your ways acknowledge Him, and He will direct your paths. Do not be wise in your own eyes; fear the Lord and depart from evil. It will be health to your body, and strength to your bones.

—Proverbs 3:5–8

If any of you lacks wisdom, let him ask of God, who gives to all men liberally and without criticism, and it will be given to him. But let him ask in faith, without wavering. For he who wavers is like a wave of the sea, driven and tossed with the wind. Let not that man think that he will receive anything from the Lord.

—James 1:5–7

DREAMS AND VISIONS

Where there is no vision, the people perish; but happy is he who keeps the teaching.

—Proverbs 29:18

As for these four youths, God gave them knowledge and skill in every branch of learning and wisdom. And Daniel had understanding in all kinds of visions and dreams.

—Daniel 1:17

And it will be that, afterwards, I will pour out My Spirit on all flesh; then your sons and your daughters will prophesy, your old men will dream dreams, and your young men will see visions.

—Joel 2:28

Surely the Lord God does nothing without revealing His purpose to His servants the prophets.

—Amos 3:7

When they did not find His body, they returned saying that they had even seen a vision of angels, who said that He was alive.

—Luke 24:23

"In the last days it shall be," says God, "that I will pour out My Spirit on all flesh; your sons and your daughters shall prophesy, your young men shall see visions, and your old men shall dream dreams. Even on My menservants and maidservants I will pour out My Spirit in those days; and they shall prophesy."

—Acts 2:17–18

EGO

Do you see a man wise in his own conceit? There is more hope for a fool than for him.

—Proverbs 26:12

The sluggard is wiser in his own conceit than seven men who can answer reasonably.

—Proverbs 26:16

I can do nothing of Myself. As I hear, I judge. My judgment is just, because I seek not My own will, but the will of the Father who sent Me. If I bear witness of Myself, My testimony is not true.

—John 5:30–31

Be of the same mind toward one another. Do not be haughty, but associate with the lowly. Do not pretend to be wiser than you are.

—Romans 12:16

Love suffers long and is kind; love envies not; love flaunts not itself and is not puffed up, does not behave itself improperly, seeks not its own, is not easily provoked, thinks no evil.

—1 Corinthians 13:4–5

Let nothing be done out of strife or conceit, but in humility let each esteem the other better than himself. Let each of you look not only to your own interests, but also to the interests of others. Let this mind be in you all, which was also in Christ Jesus.

—Philippians 2:3–5

EMPLOYER/EMPLOYEES

You may not oppress a hired servant that is poor and needy, whether he is one of your brothers or one of your foreigners who are in your land within your towns. You must give him his wages on that very day before the sun sets, for he is poor, and sets his heart on it, lest he cry against you to the Lord, and it be a sin to you.

—Deuteronomy 24:14–15

Therefore, everything you would like men to do to you, do also to them, for this is the Law and the Prophets.

—Matthew 7:12

Servants, obey those who are your masters according to the flesh, with fear and trembling, in sincerity of your heart, as to Christ, not serving when eyes are on you, but as pleasing men as the servants of Christ, doing the will of God from the heart, with good will doing service, as to the Lord, and not to men, knowing that whatever good thing any man does, he will receive the same from the Lord, whether he is enslaved or free.

—Ephesians 6:5–8

Servants, obey your masters in all things according to the flesh, serving not only when they are watching, as the servants of men, but in singleness of heart, fearing God. And whatever you do, do it heartily, as for the Lord and not for men.

—Colossians 3:22–23

For the Scripture says, "You shall not muzzle the ox that treads out the grain," and, "The laborer is worthy of his reward."

—1 Timothy 5:18

ENCOURAGEMENT

Heaviness in the heart of man makes it droop, but a good word makes it glad.

—Proverbs 12:25

But this I call to mind, and therefore I have hope: It is of the Lord's mercies that we are not consumed; His compassions do not fail. They are new every morning; great is Your faithfulness.

—Lamentations 3:21–23

The Lord is good to those who wait for Him, to the soul who seeks Him.

—Lamentations 3:25

Now may our Lord Jesus Christ Himself, and God our Father, who has loved us and has given us eternal consolation and good hope through grace, comfort your hearts and establish you in every good word and work.

—2 Thessalonians 2:16–17

And let us consider how to spur one another to love and to good works.

—Hebrews 10:24

ENDURANCE

No temptation has taken you except what is common to man. God is faithful, and He will not permit you to be tempted above what you can endure, but will with the temptation also make a way to escape, that you may be able to bear it.

—1 Corinthians 10:13

For this reason we also, since the day we heard it, do not cease to pray for you and to ask that you may be filled with the knowledge of His will in all wisdom and spiritual understanding; that you may walk in a manner worthy of the Lord, pleasing to all, being fruitful in every good work, and increasing in the knowledge of God, strengthened with all might according to His glorious power, enduring everything with perseverance and patience joyfully.

—Colossians 1:9–11

For you need patience, so that after you have done the will of God, you will receive the promise.

—Hebrews 10:36

My brothers, count it all joy when you fall into diverse temptations, knowing that the trying of your faith develops patience. But let patience perfect its work, that you may be perfect and complete, lacking nothing.

—James 1:2–4

Blessed is the man who endures temptation, for when he is tried, he will receive the crown of life, which the Lord has promised to those who love Him.

—James 1:12

ENEMIES

You have heard that it was said, "You shall love your neighbor and hate your enemy." But I say to you, love your enemies, bless those who curse you, do good to those who hate you, and pray for those who spitefully use you and persecute you.

—Matthew 5:43–44

Judge not, and you shall not be judged. Condemn not, and you will not be condemned. Forgive, and you shall be forgiven.

—Luke 6:37

For I am with you, and no one shall attack you and hurt you, for I have many people in this city.

—Acts 18:10

Repay no one evil for evil. Commend what is honest in the sight of all men. If it is possible, as much as it depends on you, live peaceably with all men. Beloved, do not avenge yourselves, but rather give place to God's wrath, for it is written: "Vengeance is Mine. I will repay," says the Lord.

—Romans 12:17–19

So we may boldly say, "The Lord is my helper, I will not fear. What can man do to me?"

—Hebrews 13:6

ETERNAL LIFE

We know that if our earthly house, this tent, were to be destroyed, we have an eternal building of God in the heavens, a house not made with hands.

—2 Corinthians 5:1

For the Lord Himself will descend from heaven with a shout, with the voice of the archangel, and with the trumpet call of God. And the dead in Christ will rise first.

—1 Thessalonians 4:16

But is now revealed by the appearing of our Savior, Jesus Christ, who has abolished death and has brought life and immortality to light through the gospel.

—2 Timothy 1:10

Blessed be the God and Father of our Lord Jesus Christ, who according to His abundant mercy has given us a new birth into a living hope through the resurrection of Jesus Christ from the dead.

—1 Peter 1:3

And this is the promise that He has promised us—eternal life.

—1 John 2:25

EVIL

And call on Me in the day of trouble; I will deliver you, and you will glorify Me.

—Psalm 50:15

The Lord shall protect you from all evil; He shall preserve your soul. The Lord shall preserve your going out and your coming in from now and for evermore.

—Psalm 121:7–8

The Lord said: Truly I will set you free for good purposes. Truly I will cause the enemy to entreat you in the time of evil and in the time of affliction.

—Jeremiah 15:11

You went forth to deliver Your people, to deliver Your anointed one. You wounded the head of the house of the wicked, laying him bare from head to foot.

—Habakkuk 3:13

I do not pray that You should take them out of the world, but that You should keep them from the evil one.

—John 17:15

Now we have received not the spirit of the world, but the Spirit which is of God, so that we might know the things that are freely given to us by God.

—1 Corinthians 2:12

EXPECTATIONS

The hope of the righteous will be gladness, but the expectation of the wicked will perish.

—Proverbs 10:28

For surely there is an end, and your expectation will not be cut off.

—Proverbs 23:18

For I know the plans that I have for you, says the Lord, plans for peace and not for evil, to give you a future and a hope.

—Jeremiah 29:11

Come to Me, all you who labor and are heavily burdened, and I will give you rest.

—MATTHEW 11:28

But he who unknowingly committed acts worthy of punishment shall be beaten with few stripes. For to whom much is given, of him much shall be required. And from him to whom much was entrusted, much will be asked.

—LUKE 12:48

Listen! I stand at the door and knock. If anyone hears My voice and opens the door, I will come in and dine with him, and he with Me.

—REVELATION 3:20

FAILURE

I will lift up my eyes to the hills, from where does my help come? My help comes from the LORD, who made heaven and earth.

—PSALM 121:1–2

Though I walk in the midst of trouble, You will preserve me; You stretch forth Your hand against the wrath of my enemies, and Your right hand saves me.

—PSALM 138:7

When you pass through waters, I will be with you. And through the rivers, they shall not overflow you. When you walk through the fire, you shall not be burned, nor shall the flame kindle on you.

—Isaiah 43:2

We know that all things work together for good to those who love God, to those who are called according to His purpose.

—Romans 8:28

But He said to me, "My grace is sufficient for you, for My strength is made perfect in weakness." Therefore most gladly I will boast in my weaknesses, that the power of Christ may rest upon me.

—2 Corinthians 12:9

FAITH

So then faith comes by hearing, and hearing by the word of God.

—Romans 10:17

For I say, through the grace given to me, to everyone among you, not to think of himself more highly than he ought to think, but to think with sound judgment, according to the measure of faith God has distributed to every man.

—Romans 12:3

For by grace you have been saved through faith, and this is not of yourselves. It is the gift of God.

—Ephesians 2:8

And that Christ may dwell in your hearts through faith; that you, being rooted and grounded in love, may be able to comprehend with all saints what is the breadth and length and depth and height, and to know the love of Christ which surpasses knowledge; that you may be filled with all the fullness of God.

—Ephesians 3:17–19

Now faith is the substance of things hoped for, the evidence of things not seen.

—Hebrews 11:1

FAME

The lips of the wise disperse knowledge, but the heart of the foolish does not do so.

—Proverbs 15:7

Better is the poor who walks in his integrity than he who is perverse in his lips and is a fool.

—Proverbs 19:1

Better is the poor who walks in his uprightness than he who is perverse in his ways, though he be rich.

—Proverbs 28:6

I urge you therefore, brothers, by the mercies of God, that you present your bodies as a living sacrifice, holy, and acceptable to God, which is your reasonable service of worship.

—Romans 12:1

In all things presenting yourself as an example of good works: in doctrine showing integrity, gravity, incorruptibility.

—Titus 2:7

For "All flesh is as grass, and all the glory of man as the flower of grass. The grass withers, and its flower falls away."

—1 Peter 1:24

FEAR

I sought the Lord, and He answered me, and delivered me from all my fears.

—Psalm 34:4

God is our refuge and strength, a well-proven help in trouble.

—Psalm 46:1

In the day the Lord gives you rest from your sorrow, and from your fear, and from the hard bondage in which you were made to serve.

—Isaiah 14:3

Be anxious for nothing, but in everything, by prayer and supplication with gratitude, make your requests known to God. And the peace of God, which surpasses all understanding, will protect your hearts and minds through Christ Jesus.

—Philippians 4:6–7

"For the eyes of the Lord are on the righteous, and His ears are open to their prayers; but the face of the Lord is against those who do evil." Who is he who will harm you if you follow that which is good? But even if you suffer for the sake of righteousness, you are blessed. "Do not be afraid of their terror, do not be troubled."

—1 Peter 3:12–14

FINANCIAL TROUBLE

How long will you sleep, O sluggard? When will you arise out of your sleep? Yet a little sleep, a little slumber, a little folding of the hands to sleep—so will your poverty come upon you like a stalker, and your need as an armed man.

—Proverbs 6:9–11

Bring all the tithes into the storehouse, that there may be food in My house, and test Me now in this, says the Lord of Hosts, if I will not open for you the windows of heaven and pour out for you a blessing, that there will not be room enough to receive it. I will rebuke the devourer for your sakes, so that it will not destroy the fruit of your ground, and the vines in your field will not fail to bear fruit, says the Lord of Hosts.

—Malachi 3:10–11

But this I say: He who sows sparingly will also reap sparingly, and he who sows bountifully will also reap bountifully. Let every man give according to the purposes in his heart, not grudgingly or out of necessity, for God loves a cheerful giver. God is able to make all grace abound toward you, so that you, always having enough of everything, may abound to every good work.

—2 Corinthians 9:6–8

I do not speak because I have need, for I have learned in whatever state I am to be content. I know both how to face humble circumstances and how to have abundance. Everywhere and in all things I have learned the secret, both to be full and to be hungry, both to abound and to suffer need. I can do all things because of Christ who strengthens me.

—Philippians 4:11–13

But my God shall supply your every need according to His riches in glory by Christ Jesus.

—Philippians 4:19

Let your lives be without love of money, and be content with the things you have. For He has said: "I will never leave you, nor forsake you." So we may boldly say: "The Lord is my helper; I will not fear. What can man do to me?"

—Hebrews 13:5–6

FLATTERY

The Lord will cut off all flattering lips, and the tongue that speaks proud things.

—Psalm 12:3

An oracle within my heart about the transgression of the wicked: There is no fear of God before their eyes. For they flatter themselves in their own eyes, that their iniquity cannot be found out and hated.

—Psalm 36:1–2

He who goes about as a talebearer reveals secrets; therefore do not meddle with him who flatters with his lips.

—Proverbs 20:19

A man who flatters his neighbor spreads a net for his feet.

—Proverbs 29:5

For there shall be no more any vain vision or flattering divination within the house of Israel.

—Ezekiel 12:24

For such people do not serve our Lord Jesus Christ, but their own appetites, and through smooth talk and flattery they deceive the hearts of the unsuspecting.

—Romans 16:18

FORGIVENESS

Blessed is he whose transgression is forgiven, whose sin is covered. Blessed is the man against whom the Lord does not count iniquity, and in whose spirit there is no deceit.

—Psalm 32:1–2

Have mercy on me, O God, according to Your lovingkindness; according to the abundance of Your compassion, blot out my transgressions. Wash me thoroughly from my iniquity, and cleanse me from my sin.

—Psalm 51:1–2

He who covers his sins will not prosper, but whoever confesses and forsakes them will have mercy.

—Proverbs 28:13

Come now, and let us reason together, says the Lord. Though your sins be as scarlet, they shall be as white as snow; though they be red like crimson, they shall be as wool.

—Isaiah 1:18

But I say to you, love your enemies, bless those who curse you, do good to those who hate you, and pray for those who spitefully use you and persecute you, that you may be sons of your Father who is in heaven. For He makes His sun rise on the evil and on the good and sends rain on the just and on the unjust.

—Matthew 5:44–45

FRIENDSHIP

A friend loves at all times, and a brother is born for adversity.

—Proverbs 17:17

A man who has friends must show himself friendly, and there is a friend who sticks closer than a brother.

—Proverbs 18:24

Make no friendship with an angry man, and with a furious man you will not go, lest you learn his ways and get a snare to your soul.

—Proverbs 22:24–25

Two are better than one, because there is a good reward for their labor together. For if they fall, then one will help up his companion. But woe to him who is alone when he falls and has no one to help him up.

—Ecclesiastes 4:9–10

A new commandment I give to you, that you love one another, even as I have loved you, that you also love one another.

—John 13:34

FRUSTRATION

Many are the afflictions of the righteous, but the Lord delivers him out of them all.

—Psalm 34:19

Do not fear, for I am with you; do not be dismayed, for I am your God. I will strengthen you, I will help you, yes, I will uphold you with My righteous right hand.

—Isaiah 41:10

And I will make an everlasting covenant with them that I will not turn away from them, to do them good. But I will put My fear in their hearts so that they shall not depart from Me.

—Jeremiah 32:40

Come to Me, all you who labor and are heavily burdened, and I will give you rest. Take My yoke upon you, and learn from Me. For I am meek and lowly in heart, and you will find rest for your souls.

—Matthew 11:28–29

What then shall we say to these things? If God is for us, who can be against us? He who did not spare His own Son, but delivered Him up for us all, how shall He not with Him also freely give us all things?

—Romans 8:31–32

FULFILLMENT

The Lord is my shepherd; I shall not want. He makes me lie down in green pastures; He leads me beside still waters. He restores my soul; He leads me in paths of righteousness for His name's sake. Even though I walk through the valley of the shadow of death, I will fear no evil; for You are with me; Your rod and Your staff, they comfort me. You prepare a table before me in the presence of my enemies; You anoint my head with oil; my cup runs over. Surely goodness and mercy shall follow me all the days of my life, and I will dwell in the house of the Lord forever.

—Psalm 23:1–6

The eyes of all wait upon You, and You give them their food in due season. You open Your hand and satisfy the desire of every living thing.

—Psalm 145:15–16

While we were yet weak, in due time Christ died for the ungodly. Rarely for a righteous man will one die. Yet perhaps for a good man some would even dare to die. But God demonstrates His own love toward us, in that while we were yet sinners, Christ died for us.

—ROMANS 5:6–8

His divine power has given to us all things that pertain to life and godliness through the knowledge of Him who has called us by His own glory and excellence, by which He has given to us exceedingly great and precious promises, so that through these things you might become partakers of the divine nature and escape the corruption that is in the world through lust.

—2 PETER 1:3–4

"This is the covenant that I will make with them after those days, says the Lord: I will put My laws into their hearts, and in their minds I will write them," then He adds, "Their sins and lawless deeds will I remember no more."

—HEBREWS 10:16–17

FUTURE

A man's heart devises his way, but the LORD directs his steps.

—PROVERBS 16:9

Do not fear, for I am with you; do not be dismayed, for I am your God. I will strengthen you, I will help you, yes, I will uphold you with My righteous right hand…I will open rivers in high places, and fountains in the midst of the valleys; I will make the wilderness a pool of water, and the dry land springs of water.

—Isaiah 41:10, 18

For I know the plans that I have for you, says the Lord, plans for peace and not for evil, to give you a future and a hope.

—Jeremiah 29:11

In My Father's house are many dwelling places. If it were not so, I would have told you. I am going to prepare a place for you. And if I go and prepare a place for you, I will come again and receive you to Myself, that where I am, you may be also.

—John 14:2–3

I have told you these things so that in Me you may have peace. In the world you will have tribulation. But be of good cheer. I have overcome the world.

—John 16:33

GAMBLING

He who loves money will not be satisfied with money; nor he who loves abundance with increase. This also is vanity.

—Ecclesiastes 5:10

No one can serve two masters. For either he will hate the one and love the other, or else he will hold to the one and despise the other. You cannot serve God and money.

—Matthew 6:24

Then He said to them, "Take heed and beware of covetousness. For a man's life does not consist in the abundance of his possessions."

—Luke 12:15

But those who desire to be rich fall into temptation and a snare and into many foolish and harmful lusts, which drown men in ruin and destruction. For the love of money is the root of all evil. While coveting after money, some have strayed from the faith and pierced themselves through with many sorrows.

—1 Timothy 6:9–10

Let your lives be without love of money, and be content with the things you have. For He has said: "I will never leave you, nor forsake you."

—Hebrews 13:5

GENEROSITY

There is one who scatters, yet increases; and there is one who withholds more than is right, but it leads to poverty. The generous soul will be made rich, and he who waters will be watered also himself.

—Proverbs 11:24–25

And whoever gives even a cup of cold water to one of these little ones in the name of a disciple, truly I tell you, he shall in no way lose his reward.

—Matthew 10:42

Give, and it will be given to you: Good measure, pressed down, shaken together, and running over will men give unto you. For with the measure you use, it will be measured unto you.

—Luke 6:38

He looked up and saw the rich putting their gifts in the treasury. He also saw a poor widow putting in two mites, and He said, "Truly I tell you, this poor widow has put in more than all of them. For all these out of their abundance have put in their gifts for God. But she out of her poverty has put in all the living she had."

—Luke 21:1–4

In all things I have shown you how, working like this, you must help the weak, remembering the words of the Lord Jesus, how He said, "It is more blessed to give than to receive."

—Acts 20:35

GIFTS FROM GOD

We have diverse gifts according to the grace that is given to us: if prophecy, according to the proportion of faith.

—Romans 12:6

There are various gifts, but the same Spirit. There are differences of administrations, but the same Lord. There are various operations, but it is the same God who operates all of them in all people. But the manifestation of the Spirit is given to everyone for the common good.

—1 Corinthians 12:4–7

So, seeing that you are zealous of spiritual gifts, seek that you may excel to the edifying of the church.

—1 Corinthians 14:12

Do not neglect the gift that is in you, which was given to you by prophecy, with the laying on of hands by the elders.

—1 Timothy 4:14

Every good gift and every perfect gift is from above and comes down from the Father of lights, with whom is no change or shadow of turning.

—James 1:17

GIVING

Do not withhold good from those to whom it is due, when it is in the power of your hand to do it.

—Proverbs 3:27

Will a man rob God? Yet you have robbed Me. But you say, "How have we robbed You?" In tithes and offerings.

—Malachi 3:8

And whoever gives even a cup of cold water to one of these little ones in the name of a disciple, truly I tell you, he shall in no way lose his reward.

—Matthew 10:42

Give, and it will be given to you: Good measure, pressed down, shaken together, and running over will men give unto you. For with the measure you use, it will be measured unto you.

—Luke 6:38

In all things I have shown you how, working like this, you must help the weak, remembering the words of the Lord Jesus, how He said, "It is more blessed to give than to receive."

—Acts 20:35

GOALS

Delight yourself in the Lord, and He will give you the desires of your heart. Commit your way to the Lord; trust also in Him, and He will bring it to pass.

—Psalm 37:4–5

But seek first the kingdom of God and His righteousness, and all these things shall be given to you.

—Matthew 6:33

Do you not know that all those who run in a race run, but one receives the prize? So run, that you may obtain it. Everyone who strives for the prize exercises self-control in all things.

Now they do it to obtain a corruptible crown, but we an incorruptible one.

—1 Corinthians 9:24–25

And let us not grow weary in doing good, for in due season we shall reap, if we do not give up.

—Galatians 6:9

Now the goal of this command is love from a pure heart, and from a good conscience, and from sincere faith.

—1 Timothy 1:5

GOD HEARS OUR PRAYERS

I called on You, for You will answer me, O God; incline Your ear to me, and hear my speech. Show marvelously Your lovingkindness, O Deliverer of those who seek refuge by Your right hand from those who arise in opposition. Keep me as the apple of Your eye; hide me under the shadow of Your wings, from the wicked who bring ruin to me, from my deadly enemies who surround me.

—Psalm 17:6–9

I will bless the Lord at all times; His praise will continually be in my mouth. My soul will make its boast in the Lord; the humble will hear of it and be glad. Oh, magnify the Lord with me, and let us exalt His name together. I sought the Lord, and He answered me, and delivered me from all my fears.

—Psalm 34:1–4

I will make them and the places all around My hill a blessing. And I will cause the showers to come down in their season. They shall be showers of blessing.

—EZEKIEL 34:26

We know that God does not listen to sinners. But if anyone is a worshipper of God and does His will, He hears him.

—JOHN 9:31

This is the confidence that we have in Him, that if we ask anything according to His will, He hears us. So if we know that He hears whatever we ask, we know that we have whatever we asked of Him.

—1 JOHN 5:14–15

GOD'S BLESSING

I will make of you a great nation; I will bless you and make your name great, so that you will be a blessing. I will bless them who bless you and curse him who curses you, and in you all families of the earth will be blessed.

—GENESIS 12:2–3

For I, the LORD your God, will hold your right hand, saying to you, "Do not fear; I will help you."

—ISAIAH 41:13

For I will pour water on him who is thirsty, and floods on the dry ground; I will pour out My Spirit on your descendants, and My blessing on your offspring.

—Isaiah 44:3

God is able to make all grace abound toward you, so that you, always having enough of everything, may abound to every good work. As it is written: "He has dispersed abroad, He has given to the poor; His righteousness remains forever." Now He who supplies seed to the sower and supplies bread for your food will also multiply your seed sown and increase the fruits of your righteousness.

—2 Corinthians 9:8–10

Blessed be the God and Father of our Lord Jesus Christ, who has blessed us with every spiritual blessing in the heavenly places in Christ.

—Ephesians 1:3

GOD'S CARE

The Lord is my shepherd; I shall not want. He makes me lie down in green pastures; He leads me beside still waters. He restores my soul; He leads me in paths of righteousness for His name's sake.

—Psalm 23:1–3

O Lord, You have searched me and known me. You know when I sit down and when I get up; You understand my thought from far off. You search my path and my lying down and are aware of all my ways.

—Psalm 139:1–3

Are not two sparrows sold for a penny? And not one of them will fall to the ground without your Father. But the very hairs of your head are all numbered. Therefore do not fear. You are more valuable than many sparrows.

—Matthew 10:29–31

If you remain in Me, and My words remain in you, you will ask whatever you desire, and it shall be done for you.

—John 15:7

Every good gift and every perfect gift is from above and comes down from the Father of lights, with whom is no change or shadow of turning.

—James 1:17

GOD'S FAITHFULNESS

Your mercy, O Lord, is in the heavens, and Your faithfulness reaches to the clouds.

—Psalm 36:5

He will send from heaven and save me from the taunt of the one who crushes me. Selah God will send forth His mercy and His truth.

—Psalm 57:3

Do not let mercy and truth forsake you; bind them around your neck, write them on the tablet of your heart, so will you find favor and good understanding in the sight of God and man.

—Proverbs 3:3–4

A faithful man will abound with blessings, but he who makes haste to be rich will not be innocent.

—Proverbs 28:20

For all the promises of God in Him are "Yes," and in Him "Amen," to the glory of God through us.

—2 Corinthians 1:20

But the fruit of the Spirit is love, joy, peace, patience, gentleness, goodness, faith, meekness, and self-control; against such there is no law.

—Galatians 5:22–23

GOD'S FAVOR

May God be gracious to us, and bless us, and cause His face to shine on us; Selah…God will bless us, and all the ends of the earth will fear Him.

—Psalm 67:1, 7

No weapon that is formed against you shall prosper, and every tongue that shall rise against you in judgment, you shall condemn. This is the heritage of the servants of the Lord, and their vindication is from Me, says the Lord.

—Isaiah 54:17

Blessed be the God and Father of our Lord Jesus Christ, who has blessed us with every spiritual blessing in the heavenly places in Christ.

—Ephesians 1:3

And above all, taking the shield of faith, with which you will be able to extinguish all the fiery arrows of the evil one.

—Ephesians 6:16

You are of God, little children, and have overcome them, because He who is in you is greater than he who is in the world.

—1 John 4:4

GOD'S LOVE

He will love you and bless you and multiply you. He will also bless the fruit of your womb and the fruit of your land, your grain, and your wine, and your oil, the increase of your herd and the young of your flock, in the land which He swore to your fathers to give you.

—Deuteronomy 7:13

The Lord opens the eyes of the blind; the Lord raises those who are brought down; the Lord loves the righteous.

—Psalm 146:8

The way of the wicked is an abomination unto the Lord, but He loves him who follows after righteousness.

—Proverbs 15:9

For as a young man marries a virgin, so your sons shall marry you; and as the bridegroom rejoices over the bride, so your God shall rejoice over you.

—Isaiah 62:5

The Lord has appeared to him from afar, saying: Indeed, I have loved you with an everlasting love; therefore with loving-kindness I have drawn you.

—Jeremiah 31:3

Indeed, I will rejoice over them to do them good, and I will plant them in this land assuredly with My whole heart and with My whole soul.

—Jeremiah 32:41

GOD'S POWER

The Lord shall fight for you, while you hold your peace.

—Exodus 14:14

Yours, O Lord, is the greatness, and the power, and the glory, and the victory, and the majesty, for everything in the heavens and the earth is Yours. Yours is the kingdom, O Lord, and You exalt Yourself as head above all.

—1 Chronicles 29:11

The LORD is my strength and my shield; my heart trusted in Him, and I was helped; therefore my heart rejoices, and with my song I will thank Him.

—PSALM 28:7

Be still and know that I am God; I will be exalted among the nations, I will be exalted in the earth.

—PSALM 46:10

For by Him all things were created that are in heaven and that are in earth, visible and invisible, whether they are thrones, or dominions, or principalities, or powers. All things were created by Him and for Him.

—COLOSSIANS 1:16

GOD'S PRESENCE

And He said, "My presence will go with you, and I will give you rest."

—EXODUS 33:14

Be strong and of a good courage. Fear not, nor be afraid of them, for the LORD your God, it is He who goes with you. He will not fail you, nor forsake you.

—DEUTERONOMY 31:6

You shall seek Me and find Me, when you shall search for Me with all your heart.

—JEREMIAH 29:13

Draw near to God, and He will draw near to you. Cleanse your hands, you sinners, and purify your hearts, you double-minded.

—James 4:8

Listen! I stand at the door and knock. If anyone hears My voice and opens the door, I will come in and dine with him, and he with Me.

—Revelation 3:20

GOD'S PROTECTION

I will say of the Lord, "He is my refuge and my fortress, my God in whom I trust." Surely He shall deliver you from the snare of the hunter and from the deadly pestilence. He shall cover you with His feathers, and under His wings you shall find protection; His faithfulness shall be your shield and wall.

—Psalm 91:2–4

They shall be Mine, says the Lord of Hosts, on the day when I make up My jewels. And I will spare them as a man spares his son who serves him.

—Malachi 3:17

For truly I say to you, whoever says to this mountain, "Be removed and be thrown into the sea," and does not doubt in his heart, but believes that what he says will come to pass, he will have whatever he says. Therefore I say to you, whatever things you ask when you pray, believe that you will receive them, and you will have them.

—Mark 11:23–24

Therefore take up the whole armor of God that you may be able to resist in the evil day, and having done all, to stand.

—Ephesians 6:13

There is no fear in love, but perfect love casts out fear, because fear has to do with punishment. Whoever fears is not perfect in love.

—1 John 4:18

GOD'S WILL

Trust in the Lord with all your heart, and lean not on your own understanding; in all your ways acknowledge Him, and He will direct your paths.

—Proverbs 3:5–6

But seek first the kingdom of God and His righteousness, and all these things shall be given to you. Therefore, take no thought about tomorrow, for tomorrow will take thought about the things of itself. Sufficient to the day is the trouble thereof.

—Matthew 6:33–34

For God is the One working in you, both to will and to do His good pleasure.

—Philippians 2:13

Rejoice always. Pray without ceasing. In everything give thanks, for this is the will of God in Christ Jesus concerning you.

—1 Thessalonians 5:16–18

In everything give thanks, for this is the will of God in Christ Jesus concerning you.

—1 Thessalonians 5:18

Come now, you who say, "Today or tomorrow we will go into this city, spend a year there, buy and sell, and make a profit," whereas you do not know what will happen tomorrow. What is your life? It is just a vapor that appears for a little while and then vanishes away. Instead you ought to say, "If the Lord wills, we shall live and do this or that."

—James 4:13–15

GOSSIP

These six things the Lord hates, yes, seven are an abomination to him: a proud look, a lying tongue, and hands that shed innocent blood, a heart that devises wicked imaginations, feet that are swift in running to mischief, a false witness who speaks lies, and he who sows discord among brethren.

—Proverbs 6:16–19

He who goes about as a talebearer reveals secrets; therefore do not meddle with him who flatters with his lips.

—Proverbs 20:19

Where there is no wood, the fire goes out; so where there is no talebearer, the strife ceases. As charcoal is to burning coals, and wood to fire, so is a contentious man to kindle strife.

—Proverbs 26:20–21

Do unto others as you would have others do unto you.

—Luke 6:31

If anyone among you seems to be religious and does not bridle his tongue, but deceives his own heart, this man's religion is vain.

—James 1:26

GRACE

We have all received from His fullness grace upon grace. For the law was given through Moses; grace and truth came through Jesus Christ. No one has seen God at any time. The only Son, who is at the Father's side, has made Him known.

—John 1:16–18

There is therefore now no condemnation for those who are in Christ Jesus, who walk not according to the flesh, but according to the Spirit.

—Romans 8:1

God is able to make all grace abound toward you, so that you, always having enough of everything, may abound to every good work.

—2 Corinthians 9:8

Because if you return to the Lord, your brothers and children will find compassion before those who have taken them captive, in order to return you to this land. For the Lord your God is gracious and compassionate. He will not turn His face from you if you all return to Him.

—2 Chronicles 30:9

Grace and peace be multiplied to you through the knowledge of God and of Jesus our Lord. His divine power has given to us all things that pertain to life and godliness through the knowledge of Him who has called us by His own glory and excellence.

—2 Peter 1:2–3

GUIDANCE

This Book of the Law must not depart from your mouth. Meditate on it day and night so that you may act carefully according to all that is written in it. For then you will make your way successful, and you will be wise.

—Joshua 1:8

Make me to know Your ways, O Lord; teach me Your paths. Lead me in Your truth and teach me, for You are the God of my salvation; on You I wait all the day.

—Psalm 25:4–5

Your word is a lamp to my feet, and a light to my path.

—Psalm 119:105

Incline your ear and hear the words of the wise, and apply your heart to my knowledge; for it is a pleasant thing if you keep them within you; they will readily be fitted in your lips. That your trust may be in the LORD, I have made known to you this day, even to you.

—PROVERBS 22:17–19

And the LORD shall guide you continually, and satisfy your soul in drought, and strengthen your bones; and you shall be like a watered garden, and like a spring of water, whose waters do not fail.

—ISAIAH 58:11

GUILT

I will cleanse them from all their iniquity whereby they have sinned against Me. And I will pardon all their iniquities whereby they have sinned and whereby they have transgressed against Me.

—JEREMIAH 33:8

There is therefore now no condemnation for those who are in Christ Jesus, who walk not according to the flesh, but according to the Spirit.

—ROMANS 8:1

Therefore, if any man is in Christ, he is a new creature. Old things have passed away. Look, all things have become new.

—2 CORINTHIANS 5:17

But if we walk in the light as He is in the light, we have fellowship one with another, and the blood of Jesus Christ His Son cleanses us from all sin.

—1 John 1:7

If we confess our sins, He is faithful and just to forgive us our sins and cleanse us from all unrighteousness.

—1 John 1:9

HABITS

If I have walked in vanity, or if my foot has hurried after deceit, let me be weighed in an even balance that God may know my integrity.

—Job 31:5–6

Put away from you a deceitful mouth, and put perverse lips far from you. Let your eyes look right on, and let your eyelids look straight before you. Ponder the path of your feet, and let all your ways be established. Do not turn to the right or to the left; remove your foot from evil.

—Proverbs 4:24–27

Do not be conformed to this world, but be transformed by the renewing of your mind, that you may prove what is the good and acceptable and perfect will of God.

—Romans 12:2

"All things are lawful to me," but not all things are helpful. "All things are lawful for me," but I will not be brought under the power of anything.

—1 Corinthians 6:12

No temptation has taken you except what is common to man. God is faithful, and He will not permit you to be tempted above what you can endure, but will with the temptation also make a way to escape, that you may be able to bear it.

—1 Corinthians 10:13

HEALING

He said, "If you diligently listen to the voice of the Lord your God, and do what is right in His sight, and give ear to His commandments, and keep all His statutes, I will not afflict you with any of the diseases with which I have afflicted the Egyptians. For I am the Lord who heals you."

—Exodus 15:26

The Lord will sustain them on the sickbed; You will restore all his lying down in his illness.

—Psalm 41:3

But he was wounded for our transgressions, he was bruised for our iniquities; the chastisement of our peace was upon him, and by his stripes we are healed.

—Isaiah 53:5

To fulfill what was spoken by Isaiah the prophet, "He Himself took our infirmities and bore our sicknesses."

—Matthew 8:17

And whatever we ask, we will receive from Him, because we keep His commandments and do the things that are pleasing in His sight. And this is His commandment: that we should believe on the name of His Son Jesus Christ and love one another as He commanded us.

—1 John 3:22–23

HEAVEN

In My Father's house are many dwelling places. If it were not so, I would have told you. I am going to prepare a place for you. And if I go and prepare a place for you, I will come again and receive you to Myself, that where I am, you may be also.

—John 14:2–3

For Christ did not enter holy places made with hands, which are patterned after the true one, but into heaven itself, now to appear in the presence of God for us.

—Hebrews 9:24

But they desired a better country, that is, a heavenly one. Therefore God is not ashamed to be called their God, for He has prepared a city for them.

—Hebrews 11:16

Beloved, now are we sons of God, and it has not yet been revealed what we shall be. But we know that when He appears, we shall be like Him, for we shall see Him as He is.

—1 John 3:2

Then I looked. And there was a great multitude which no one could count, from all nations and tribes and peoples and tongues, standing before the throne and before the Lamb, clothed with white robes, with palm branches in their hands.

—Revelation 7:9

I saw no temple in the city, for the Lord God Almighty and the Lamb are its temple. The city has no need of sun or moon to shine in it, for the glory of God is its light, and its lamp is the Lamb. And the nations of those who are saved shall walk in its light, and the kings of the earth shall bring their glory and honor into it.

—Revelation 21:22–24

HELP IN TROUBLES

The Lord also will be a refuge for the oppressed, a refuge in times of trouble.

—Psalm 9:9

The Lord is my pillar, and my fortress, and my deliverer; my God, my rock, in whom I take refuge; my shield, and the horn of my salvation, my high tower.

—Psalm 18:2

The Lord is my strength and my shield; my heart trusted in Him, and I was helped; therefore my heart rejoices, and with my song I will thank Him.

—Psalm 28:7

You are my hiding place; You will preserve me from trouble; You will surround me with shouts of deliverance. Selah

—Psalm 32:7

Why, my soul, are you cast down? Why do you groan within me? Wait for God; I will yet thank Him, For He is my deliverance and my God.

—Psalm 42:11

Cast your burden on the Lord, and He will sustain you; He will never allow the righteous to be moved.

—Psalm 55:22

HOLINESS

Only carefully obey the commandment and the law that Moses the servant of the Lord commanded you: to love the Lord your God, to walk in all His ways, to obey His commandments, to cling to Him, and to serve Him with all your heart and soul.

—Joshua 22:5

But now, having been freed from sin and having become slaves of God, you have fruit unto holiness, and the end is eternal life.

—Romans 6:22

Since we have these promises, beloved, let us cleanse ourselves from all filthiness of the flesh and spirit, perfecting holiness in the fear of God.

—2 Corinthians 7:1

That you put off the former way of life in the old nature, which is corrupt according to the deceitful lusts, and be renewed in the spirit of your mind; and that you put on the new nature, which was created according to God in righteousness and true holiness.

—Ephesians 4:22–24

For they indeed disciplined us for a short time according to their own judgment, but He does so for our profit, that we may partake of His holiness.

—Hebrews 12:10

HOLY SPIRIT

As for Me, this is My covenant with them, says the Lord: My Spirit who is upon you, and My words which I have put in your mouth shall not depart out of your mouth, nor out of the mouth of your descendants, nor out of the mouth of your descendants' descendants, says the Lord, from this time forth and forever.

—Isaiah 59:21

I will put My Spirit within you and cause you to walk in My statutes, and you will keep My judgments and do them.

—Ezekiel 36:27

I will pray the Father, and He will give you another Counselor, that He may be with you forever: the Spirit of truth, whom the world cannot receive, for it does not see Him, neither does it know Him. But you know Him, for He lives with you, and will be in you.

—John 14:16–17

Peter said to them, "Repent and be baptized, every one of you, in the name of Jesus Christ for the forgiveness of sins, and you shall receive the gift of the Holy Spirit."

—Acts 2:38

Likewise, the Spirit helps us in our weaknesses, for we do not know what to pray for as we ought, but the Spirit Himself intercedes for us with groanings too deep for words. He who searches the hearts knows what the mind of the Spirit is, because He intercedes for the saints according to the will of God.

—Romans 8:26–27

HONESTY

Make me to know Your ways, O Lord; teach me Your paths. Lead me in Your truth and teach me, for You are the God of my salvation; on You I wait all the day.

—Psalm 25:4–5

He who walks righteously and speaks uprightly, he who rejects unjust gain and shakes his hands from holding bribes, who stops his ears from hearing of bloodshed, and shuts his eyes from seeing evil: He shall dwell on high; his place of defense shall be the impregnable rock; his bread shall be given him, his waters shall be sure.

—Isaiah 33:15–16

These are the things you will do: Speak truth each to his neighbor, and make judgments in your gates that are for truth, and justice, and peace.

—Zechariah 8:16

He who is faithful in what is least is faithful also in much. And he who is dishonest in the least is dishonest also in much.

—Luke 16:10

Do not lie one to another, since you have put off the old nature with its deeds, and have embraced the new nature, which is renewed in knowledge after the image of Him who created it.

—Colossians 3:9–10

HOPE

But I will hope continually, and will add to all Your praise.

—Psalm 71:14

Blessed is he who has the God of Jacob for his help, whose hope is in the Lord his God, who made heaven, and earth, the sea, and all that is in them, who keeps faithfulness forever.

—Psalm 146:5–6

But those who wait upon the LORD shall renew their strength; they shall mount up with wings as eagles, they shall run and not be weary, and they shall walk and not faint.

—ISAIAH 40:31

Blessed is the man who trusts in the LORD, and whose hope is the LORD. For he shall be as a tree planted by the waters, and that spreads out its roots by the river, and shall not fear when heat comes, but its leaf shall be green, and it shall not be anxious in the year of drought, neither shall cease from yielding fruit.

—JEREMIAH 17:7–8

Now may the God of hope fill you with all joy and peace in believing, so that you may abound in hope, through the power of the Holy Spirit.

—ROMANS 15:13

HOW TO BE BORN AGAIN

He then led them out and asked, "Sirs, what must I do to be saved?" They said, "Believe in the Lord Jesus Christ, and you and your household will be saved."

—ACTS 16:30–31

There is therefore now no condemnation for those who are in Christ Jesus, who walk not according to the flesh, but according to the Spirit.

—ROMANS 8:1

For the Scripture says, "Whoever believes in Him will not be ashamed."

—Romans 10:11

Now, brothers, I declare to you the gospel which I preached to you, which you have received, and in which you stand. Through it you are saved, if you keep in memory what I preached to you, unless you have believed in vain.

—1 Corinthians 15:1–2

He Himself bore our sins in His own body on the tree, that we, being dead to sins, should live unto righteousness. "By His wounds you were healed."

—1 Peter 2:24

HUMILITY

If My people, who are called by My name, will humble themselves and pray, and seek My face and turn from their wicked ways, then I will hear from heaven, and will forgive their sin and will heal their land.

—2 Chronicles 7:14

The desire of the humble You have heard, O Lord; You make their heart attentive; You bend Your ear.

—Psalm 10:17

The fear of the Lord is the instruction of wisdom, and before honor is humility.

—Proverbs 15:33

Better it is to be of a humble spirit with the lowly than to divide the spoil with the proud.

—Proverbs 16:19

I tell you, this man went down to his house justified rather than the other. For everyone who exalts himself will be humbled, and he who humbles himself will be exalted.

—Luke 18:14

But He gives more grace. For this reason it says, "God resists the proud, but gives grace to the humble."

—James 4:6

HYPOCRISY

For there is no uprightness in their mouth; destruction is in their midst; their throat is an open tomb; they flatter with their tongue.

—Psalm 5:9

Therefore, the Lord said: Because this people draw near with their mouths and honor Me with their lips, but have removed their hearts far from Me, and their fear toward Me is tradition by the precept of men.

—Isaiah 29:13

You hypocrite! First take the plank out of your own eye, and then you will see clearly to take the speck out of your brother's eye.

—Matthew 7:5

Why do you see the speck that is in your brother's eye, but do not see the beam that is in your own eye? How can you say to your brother, "Brother, let me remove the speck that is in your eye," when you yourself do not see the beam that is in your own eye? You hypocrite! First remove the beam from your own eye, and then you will see clearly to remove the speck that is in your brother's eye.

—Luke 6:41–42

They profess that they know God, but in their deeds they deny Him, being abominable, disobedient, and worthless for every good work.

—Titus 1:16

ILLNESS

The Lord will preserve them and keep them alive, and they will be blessed on the earth, and You will not deliver them to the will of their enemies. The Lord will sustain them on the sickbed; You will restore all his lying down in his illness. I said, "Lord, be gracious to me; heal my soul, for I have sinned against You."

—Psalm 41:2–4

To fulfill what was spoken by Isaiah the prophet, "He Himself took our infirmities and bore our sicknesses."

—Matthew 8:17

I have told you these things so that in Me you may have peace. In the world you will have tribulation. But be of good cheer. I have overcome the world.

—John 16:33

But He said to me, "My grace is sufficient for you, for My strength is made perfect in weakness." Therefore most gladly I will boast in my weaknesses, that the power of Christ may rest upon me.

—2 Corinthians 12:9

But my God shall supply your every need according to His riches in glory by Christ Jesus.

—Philippians 4:19

INTEGRITY

God forbid that I should justify you. Until I die I will not put away my integrity from me.

—Job 27:5

Truth and integrity will preserve me while I wait for You.

—Psalm 25:21

The integrity of the upright will guide them, but the perverseness of transgressors will destroy them.

—Proverbs 11:3

Providing for honest things, not only in the sight of the Lord but also in the sight of men.

—2 Corinthians 8:21

Live your lives honorably among the Gentiles, so that though they speak against you as evildoers, they shall see your good works and thereby glorify God in the day of visitation.

—1 Peter 2:12

But whoever keeps His word truly has the love of God perfected in him. By this we know we are in Him.

—1 John 2:5

JEALOUSY

Rest in the Lord, and wait patiently for Him; do not fret because of those who prosper in their way, because of those who make wicked schemes.

—Psalm 37:7

A sound heart is the life of the flesh, but envy the rottenness of the bones.

—Proverbs 14:30

Do not be envious against evil men, nor desire to be with them.

—Proverbs 24:1

Then He said to His disciples, "Therefore I say to you, do not be anxious for your life, what you will eat, nor for your body, what you will wear. Life is more than food, and the body is more than clothes."

—Luke 12:22–23

Let us not be conceited, provoking one another and envying one another.

—Galatians 5:26

But if you have bitter envying and strife in your hearts, do not boast and do not lie against the truth.

—James 3:14

JESUS CHRIST

For God so loved the world that He gave His only begotten Son, that whoever believes in Him should not perish, but have eternal life. For God did not send His Son into the world to condemn the world, but that the world through Him might be saved.

—John 3:16–17

Jesus said to her, "I am the resurrection and the life. He who believes in Me, though he may die, yet shall he live. And whoever lives and believes in Me shall never die. Do you believe this?"

—John 11:25–26

That if you confess with your mouth Jesus is Lord, and believe in your heart that God has raised Him from the dead, you will be saved.

—Romans 10:9

Therefore God highly exalted Him and gave Him the name which is above every name, that at the name of Jesus every knee should bow, of those in heaven and on earth and under the earth, and every tongue should confess that Jesus Christ is Lord, to the glory of God the Father.

—Philippians 2:9–11

For if we believe that Jesus died and arose again, so God will bring with Him those who sleep in Jesus.

—1 Thessalonians 4:14

JOY AND GLADNESS

You will make known to me the path of life; in Your presence is fullness of joy; at Your right hand there are pleasures for evermore.

—Psalm 16:11

Blessed are the people who know the joyful shout. They walk, O Lord, in the light of Your presence. In Your name they rejoice all the day, and in Your righteousness they shall be exalted.

—Psalm 89:15–16

Blessed are you when men hate you, and when they separate you from their company and insult you, and cast out your name as evil, on account of the Son of Man. Rejoice in that day, and leap for joy, for indeed, your reward is great in heaven. For in like manner their fathers treated the prophets.

—Luke 6:22–23

For the kingdom of God does not mean eating and drinking, but righteousness and peace and joy in the Holy Spirit.

—Romans 14:17

My brothers, count it all joy when you fall into diverse temptations, knowing that the trying of your faith develops patience.

—James 1:2–3

JUDGING OTHERS

Judge not, that you be not judged. For with what judgment you judge, you will be judged. And with the measure you use, it will be measured again for you. And why do you see the speck that is in your brother's eye, but do not consider the plank that is in your own eye? Or how will you say to your brother, "Let me pull the speck out of your eye," when a log is in your own eye? You hypocrite! First take the plank out of your own eye, and then you will see clearly to take the speck out of your brother's eye.

—Matthew 7:1–5

Judge not, and you shall not be judged. Condemn not, and you will not be condemned. Forgive, and you shall be forgiven.

—Luke 6:37

So when they continued asking Him, He stood up and said to them, "Let him who is without sin among you be the first to throw a stone at her."

—John 8:7

Let no unwholesome word proceed out of your mouth, but only that which is good for building up, that it may give grace to the listeners.

—Ephesians 4:29

Do not speak evil of one another, brothers. He who speaks evil of his brother and judges his brother speaks evil of the law and judges the law. If you judge the law, you are not a doer of the law, but a judge. There is one Lawgiver who is able to save and to destroy. Who are you to judge another?

—James 4:11–12

KINDNESS

Bear one another's burdens, and so fulfill the law of Christ.

—Galatians 6:2

And be kind one to another, tenderhearted, forgiving one another, just as God in Christ also forgave you.

—Ephesians 4:32

So embrace, as the elect of God, holy and beloved, a spirit of mercy, kindness, humbleness of mind, meekness, and longsuffering.

—Colossians 3:12

We also were once foolish, disobedient, deceived, serving various desires and pleasures, living in evil and envy, filled with hatred and hating each other. But when the kindness and the love of God our Savior toward mankind appeared, not by works of righteousness which we have done, but according to His mercy He saved us, through the washing of rebirth and the renewal of the Holy Spirit.

—Titus 3:3–5

Finally, be all of one mind, be loving toward one another, be gracious, and be kind. Do not repay evil for evil, or curse for curse, but on the contrary, bless, knowing that to this you are called, so that you may receive a blessing.

—1 Peter 3:8–9

KNOWLEDGE

The fear of the Lord is the beginning of knowledge, but fools despise wisdom and instruction.

—Proverbs 1:7

When wisdom enters your heart, and knowledge is pleasant to your soul.

—Proverbs 2:10

The heart of the prudent gets knowledge, and the ear of the wise seeks knowledge.

—Proverbs 18:15

The Spirit of the Lord shall rest upon him, the Spirit of wisdom and understanding, the Spirit of counsel and might, the Spirit of knowledge and of the fear of the Lord.

—Isaiah 11:2

My people are destroyed for lack of knowledge. Because you have rejected knowledge, I will reject you from being My priest. And because you have forgotten the law of your God, I will also forget your children. As they increased, so they sinned against Me. I will change their glory into shame.

—Hosea 4:6–7

LAZINESS

Yet a little sleep, a little slumber, a little folding of the hands to sleep—so will your poverty come upon you like a stalker, and your need as an armed man.

—Proverbs 6:10–11

Do not be lazy in diligence, be fervent in spirit, serve the Lord.

—Romans 12:11

Let him who steals steal no more. Instead, let him labor, working with his hands things which are good, that he may have something to share with him who is in need.

—Ephesians 4:28

Learn to be calm, and to conduct your own business, and to work with your own hands, as we commanded you, so that you may walk honestly toward those who are outsiders and that you may lack nothing.

—1 Thessalonians 4:11–12

For when we were with you, we commanded you that if any will not work, neither shall he eat. For we hear that there are some among you who live in idleness, mere busybodies, not working at all. Now, concerning those who are such, we command and exhort by our Lord Jesus Christ that they quietly work and eat their own bread.

—2 Thessalonians 3:10–12

LIFE

My son, do not forget my teaching, but let your heart keep my commandments; for length of days and long life and peace will they add to you.

—Proverbs 3:1–2

For whoever would save his life will lose it, and whoever loses his life for My sake will find it.

—Matthew 16:25

Jesus said to them, "I am the bread of life. Whoever comes to Me shall never hunger, and whoever believes in Me shall never thirst."

—John 6:35

The thief does not come, except to steal and kill and destroy. I came that they may have life, and that they may have it more abundantly.

—John 10:10

Jesus said to him, "I am the way, the truth, and the life. No one comes to the Father except through Me."

—John 14:6

His divine power has given to us all things that pertain to life and godliness through the knowledge of Him who has called us by His own glory and excellence.

—2 Peter 1:3

LISTENING

Incline your ear to wisdom, and apply your heart to understanding.

—Proverbs 2:2

He who answers a matter before he hears it, it is folly and shame to him.

—Proverbs 18:13

Hear counsel and receive instruction, that you may be wise in your latter days.

—Proverbs 19:20

He who is of God hears God's words. Therefore, you do not hear them, because you are not of God.

—John 8:47

Therefore, my beloved brothers, let every man be swift to hear, slow to speak, and slow to anger.

—James 1:19

LONG LIFE

You shall walk in all the ways which the Lord your God has commanded you, so that you may live and that it may be well with you, and that you may prolong your days in the land which you shall possess.

—Deuteronomy 5:33

"Lord, make me to know my end, and what is the measure of my days, that I may know how transient I am. Indeed, You have made my days as a handbreadth, and my age is as nothing before You; indeed every man at his best is as a breath." Selah

—Psalm 39:4–5

My son, do not forget my teaching, but let your heart keep my commandments; for length of days and long life and peace will they add to you.

—Proverbs 3:1–2

For by me your days will be multiplied, and the years of your life will be increased.

—Proverbs 9:11

And even to your old age I am He, and even to your graying years I will carry you; I have done it, and I will bear you; even I will carry, and will deliver you.

—Isaiah 46:4

LONELINESS

No man will be able to stand against you all the days of your life. As I was with Moses, I will be with you. I will not abandon you. I will not leave you.

—Joshua 1:5

But I am poor and needy; yet the Lord thinks about me. You are my help and my deliverer; do not delay, O my God.

—Psalm 40:17

A father of the fatherless, and a protector of the widows, is God in His holy habitation. God sets the deserted in families; He brings out prisoners into prosperity, but the rebellious dwell in a dry land.

—Psalm 68:5–6

I will lift up my eyes to the hills, from where comes my help? My help comes from the Lord, who made heaven and earth.

—Psalm 121:1–2

Do not fear, for I am with you; do not be dismayed, for I am your God. I will strengthen you, I will help you, yes, I will uphold you with My righteous right hand.

—Isaiah 41:10

LOVE

I love those who love me, and those who seek me early will find me.

—Proverbs 8:17

Jesus said to him, "'You shall love the Lord your God with all your heart, and with all your soul, and with all your mind.' This is the first and great commandment."

—Matthew 22:37–38

A new commandment I give to you, that you love one another, even as I have loved you, that you also love one another. By this all men will know that you are My disciples, if you have love for one another.

—John 13:34–35

Walk in love, as Christ loved us and gave Himself for us as a fragrant offering and a sacrifice to God.

—Ephesians 5:2

As concerning brotherly love, you do not need me to write to you. For you yourselves are taught by God to love one another.

—1 Thessalonians 4:9

LOVE ONE ANOTHER

This is My commandment: that you love one another, as I have loved you. Greater love has no man than this: that a man lay down his life for his friends.

—John 15:12–13

Let love be without hypocrisy. Hate what is evil. Cleave to what is good. Be devoted to one another with brotherly love; prefer one another in honor.

—Romans 12:9–10

Love suffers long and is kind; love envies not; love flaunts not itself and is not puffed up, does not behave itself improperly, seeks not its own, is not easily provoked, thinks no evil; rejoices not in iniquity, but rejoices in the truth; bears all things, believes all things, hopes all things, and endures all things. Love never fails. But if there are prophecies, they shall fail; if there are tongues, they shall cease; and if there is knowledge, it shall vanish.

—1 Corinthians 13:4–8

Therefore, as we have opportunity, let us do good to all people, especially to those who are of the household of faith.

—Galatians 6:10

If anyone says, "I love God," and hates his brother, he is a liar. For whoever does not love his brother whom he has seen, how can he love God whom he has not seen?

—1 John 4:20

LOYALTY

You shall have no other gods before Me... You shall not bow down to them or serve them; for I, the Lord your God, am a jealous God, visiting the iniquity of the fathers on the children to the third and fourth generation of them who hate Me.

—Exodus 20:3–5

O Lord, the God of Abraham, Isaac, and Israel, our fathers, keep this forever in the thoughts and intentions of the heart of Your people and direct their heart to You.

—1 Chronicles 29:18

That they might set their hope in God and not forget the works of God, but keep His commandments, and they might not be as their fathers, a stubborn and rebellious generation, a generation that did not set their heart steadfast, and whose spirit was not faithful to God.

—Psalm 78:7–8

A man who has friends must show himself friendly, and there is a friend who sticks closer than a brother.

—Proverbs 18:24

If it be so, our God whom we serve is able to deliver us from the burning fiery furnace, and He will deliver us out of your hand, O king. But even if He does not, be it known to you, O king, that we will not serve your gods, nor worship the golden image which you have set up.

—Daniel 3:17–18

LUST

Do not lust after her beauty in your heart, nor let her allure you with her eyelids. For by means of a harlot a man is reduced to a piece of bread, and the adulteress will prey upon his precious life. Can a man take fire in his bosom, and his clothes not be burned? Can one walk upon hot coals, and his feet not be burned? So he who goes in to his neighbor's wife; whoever touches her will not be innocent.

—Proverbs 6:25–29

You have heard that it was said by the ancients, "You shall not commit adultery." But I say to you that whoever looks on a woman to lust after her has committed adultery with her already in his heart.

—Matthew 5:27–28

So flee youthful desires and pursue righteousness, faith, love, and peace, with those who call on the Lord out of a pure heart.

—2 Timothy 2:22

Therefore submit yourselves to God. Resist the devil, and he will flee from you. Draw near to God, and He will draw near to you. Cleanse your hands, you sinners, and purify your hearts, you double-minded.

—James 4:7–8

As obedient children do not conduct yourselves according to the former lusts in your ignorance. But as He who has called you is holy, so be holy in all your conduct, because it is written, "Be holy, for I am holy."

—1 Peter 1:14–16

LYING

You must not give a false report. Do not join your hand with the wicked to be a malicious witness.

—Exodus 23:1

You shall not swear falsely by My name, and so defile the name of your God: I am the Lord.

—Leviticus 19:12

A man who bears false witness against his neighbor is like a club, a sword, and a sharp arrow.

—Proverbs 25:18

Do not lie one to another, since you have put off the old nature with its deeds, and have embraced the new nature, which is renewed in knowledge after the image of Him who created it.

—Colossians 3:9–10

But if you have bitter envying and strife in your hearts, do not boast and do not lie against the truth.

—James 3:14

But the cowardly, the unbelieving, the abominable, the murderers, the sexually immoral, the sorcerers, the idolaters, and all liars shall have their portion in the lake which burns with fire and brimstone. This is the second death.

—Revelation 21:8

MARRIAGE

Let your fountain be blessed, and rejoice with the wife of your youth. Let her be as the loving deer and pleasant doe; let her breasts satisfy you at all times; and always be enraptured with her love. Why should you, my son, be intoxicated by an immoral woman, and embrace the bosom of a seductress?

—Proverbs 5:18–20

Whoever finds a wife finds a good thing, and obtains favor of the Lord.

—Proverbs 18:22

Enjoy life with the wife whom you love all the days of your vain life which He has given you under the sun; because that is your reward in life and in your toil because you have labored under the sun.

—Ecclesiastes 9:9

Let the husband render to the wife due affection, and likewise the wife to the husband.

—1 Corinthians 7:3

Marriage is to be honored among everyone, and the bed undefiled. But God will judge the sexually immoral and adulterers.

—Hebrews 13:4

MATERIALISM

Do not store up for yourselves treasures on earth where moth and rust destroy and where thieves break in and steal. But store up for yourselves treasures in heaven, where neither moth nor rust destroy and where thieves do not break in nor steal, for where your treasure is, there will your heart be also.

—Matthew 6:19–21

Do not be conformed to this world, but be transformed by the renewing of your mind, that you may prove what is the good and acceptable and perfect will of God.

—Romans 12:2

But those who desire to be rich fall into temptation and a snare and into many foolish and harmful lusts, which drown men in ruin and destruction. For the love of money is the root of all evil. While coveting after money, some have strayed from the faith and pierced themselves through with many sorrows.

—1 Timothy 6:9–10

Let your lives be without love of money, and be content with the things you have. For He has said: "I will never leave you, nor forsake you."

—Hebrews 13:5

For all that is in the world—the lust of the flesh, the lust of the eyes, and the pride of life—is not of the Father, but is of the world.

—1 John 2:16

MEDITATION

This Book of the Law must not depart from your mouth. Meditate on it day and night so that you may act carefully according to all that is written in it. For then you will make your way successful, and you will be wise.

—Joshua 1:8

His delight is in the law of the Lord, and in His law he meditates day and night.

—Psalm 1:2

Let the words of my mouth and the meditation of my heart be acceptable in Your sight, O Lord, my strength and my Redeemer.

—Psalm 19:14

You will keep him in perfect peace, whose mind is stayed on You, because he trusts in You.

—Isaiah 26:3

But you, when you pray, enter your closet, and when you have shut your door, pray to your Father who is in secret. And your Father who sees in secret will reward you openly.

—Matthew 6:6

MEEKNESS

But the meek will inherit the earth, and will delight themselves in the abundance of peace.

—Psalm 37:11

But with righteousness he shall judge the poor, and reprove with fairness for the meek of the earth. He shall strike the earth with the rod of his mouth, and with the breath of his lips he shall slay the wicked.

—Isaiah 11:4

The meek also shall increase their joy in the Lord, and the poor among men shall rejoice in the Holy One of Israel.

—Isaiah 29:19

Seek the Lord, all you humble of the land, who carry out His judgment. Seek righteousness, seek humility. Perhaps you will be hidden on the day of the Lord's anger.

—Zephaniah 2:3

Blessed are the meek, for they shall inherit the earth.

—Matthew 5:5

MERCY

Then He said, "I will make all My goodness pass before you, and I will proclaim the name of the LORD before you. I will be gracious to whom I will be gracious and will show mercy on whom I will show mercy."

—Exodus 33:19

Have mercy on me, O God, according to Your lovingkindness; according to the abundance of Your compassion, blot out my transgressions.

—Psalm 51:1

Blessed are the merciful, for they shall obtain mercy.

—Matthew 5:7

His mercy is on those who fear Him from generation to generation.

—Luke 1:50

Be therefore merciful, even as your Father is merciful.

—Luke 6:36

But God, being rich in mercy, because of His great love with which He loved us, even when we were dead in sins, made us alive together with Christ (by grace you have been saved).

—Ephesians 2:4–5

MONEY

There is one who makes himself rich, yet has nothing; there is one who makes himself poor, yet has great riches.

—Proverbs 13:7

He who loves money will not be satisfied with money; nor he who loves abundance with increase. This also is vanity.

—Ecclesiastes 5:10

He who is faithful in what is least is faithful also in much. And he who is dishonest in the least is dishonest also in much. So if you have not been faithful in the unrighteous wealth, who will commit to your trust the true riches?

—Luke 16:10–11

But my God shall supply your every need according to His riches in glory by Christ Jesus.

—Philippians 4:19

For the love of money is the root of all evil. While coveting after money, some have strayed from the faith and pierced themselves through with many sorrows.

—1 Timothy 6:10

MORAL PURITY

Do you not know that the unrighteous will not inherit the kingdom of God? Do not be deceived. Neither the sexually immoral, nor idolaters, nor adulterers, nor male prostitutes, nor homosexuals, nor thieves, nor covetous, nor drunkards, nor revilers, nor extortioners will inherit the kingdom of God. Such were some of you. But you were washed, you were sanctified, and you were justified in the name of the Lord Jesus by the Spirit of our God.

—1 Corinthians 6:9–11

Now the works of the flesh are revealed, which are these: adultery, sexual immorality, impurity, lewdness, idolatry, sorcery, hatred, strife, jealousy, rage, selfishness, dissensions, heresies, envy, murders, drunkenness, carousing, and the like. I warn you, as I previously warned you, that those who do such things shall not inherit the kingdom of God.

—Galatians 5:19–21

Finally, brothers, whatever things are true, whatever things are honest, whatever things are just, whatever things are pure, whatever things are lovely, whatever things are of good report, if there is any virtue, and if there is any praise, think on these things.

—Philippians 4:8

You adulterers and adulteresses, do you not know that the friendship with the world is enmity with God? Whoever therefore will be a friend of the world is the enemy of God.

—James 4:4

But as He who has called you is holy, so be holy in all your conduct, because it is written, "Be holy, for I am holy."

—1 Peter 1:15–16

MOTIVES

Every way of a man is right in his own eyes, but the LORD weighs the hearts.

—Proverbs 21:2

Therefore judge nothing before the appointed time until the Lord comes. He will bring to light the hidden things of darkness and will reveal the purposes of the hearts. Then everyone will have commendation from God.

—1 Corinthians 4:5

For am I now seeking the approval of men or of God? Or am I trying to please men? For if I were still trying to please men, I would not be the servant of Christ.

—Galatians 1:10

Let nothing be done out of strife or conceit, but in humility let each esteem the other better than himself.

—Philippians 2:3

But as we were allowed by God to be entrusted with the gospel, even so we speak, not to please men, but God, who examines our hearts.

—1 Thessalonians 2:4

MY CALLING

You are the salt of the earth. But if the salt loses its saltiness, how shall it be made salty? It is from then on good for nothing

but to be thrown out and to be trampled underfoot by men.
You are the light of the world. A city that is set on a hill cannot
be hidden

—Matthew 5:13–14

Teaching them to observe all things I have commanded you.
And remember, I am with you always, even to the end of
the age.

—Matthew 28:20

Truly, truly I say to you, he who believes in Me will do the
works that I do also. And he will do greater works than these,
because I am going to My Father.

—John 14:12

God is faithful, and by Him you were called to the fellowship
of His Son, Jesus Christ our Lord.

—1 Corinthians 1:9

For by grace you have been saved through faith, and this is not
of yourselves. It is the gift of God, not of works, so that no one
should boast. For we are His workmanship, created in Christ
Jesus for good works, which God prepared beforehand, so that
we should walk in them.

—Ephesians 2:8–10

For God has not called us to uncleanness, but to holiness.

—1 Thessalonians 4:7

NEED CONFIDENCE

For the Lord will be your confidence, and will keep your foot from being caught.

—Proverbs 3:26

Do not fear, for I am with you; do not be dismayed, for I am your God. I will strengthen you, I will help you, yes, I will uphold you with My righteous right hand.

—Isaiah 41:10

Now may the God of hope fill you with all joy and peace in believing, so that you may abound in hope, through the power of the Holy Spirit.

—Romans 15:13

Not that we are sufficient in ourselves to take credit for anything of ourselves, but our sufficiency is from God.

—2 Corinthians 3:5

So we may boldly say, "The Lord is my helper, I will not fear. What can man do to me?"

—Hebrews 13:6

NEED COURAGE

Be strong and of a good courage. Fear not, nor be afraid of them, for the Lord your God, it is He who goes with you. He will not fail you, nor forsake you.

—Deuteronomy 31:6

Have not I commanded you? Be strong and courageous. Do not be afraid or dismayed, for the Lord your God is with you wherever you go.

—Joshua 1:9

Watch, stand fast in the faith, be bold like men, and be strong.
—1 Corinthians 16:13

Then David said to Solomon his son, "Be strong and courageous, and take action. Do not be afraid nor be dismayed for the Lord God, my God, is with you. He will not leave you nor forsake you, until you have finished all the work of the service of the house of the Lord."

—1 Chronicles 28:20

Do not be frightened by your adversaries. This is a sign to them of their destruction, but of your salvation, and this from God.

—Philippians 1:28

OBEDIENCE

See, today I have set before you life and prosperity, and death and disaster. What I am commanding you today is to love the Lord your God, to walk in His ways, and to keep His commandments and His statutes and His judgments, so that you may live and multiply. Then the Lord your God will bless you in the land which you go to possess.—Deuteronomy 30:15–16

Blessed are those who keep justice and who do righteousness at all times.

—Psalm 106:3

For whoever does the will of My Father who is in heaven is My brother, and sister, and mother.

—Matthew 12:50

And being found in the form of a man, He humbled Himself and became obedient to death, even death on a cross.

—Philippians 2:8

Whoever, therefore, breaks one of the least of these commandments and teaches others to do likewise shall be called the least in the kingdom of heaven. But whoever does and teaches them shall be called great in the kingdom of heaven.

—Matthew 5:19

OPPRESSION

He will judge the world in righteousness; He will give judgment to the peoples in uprightness. The Lord also will be a refuge for the oppressed, a refuge in times of trouble. Those who know Your name will put their trust in You, for You, Lord, have not forsaken those who seek You.

—Psalm 9:8–10

Keep me as the apple of Your eye; hide me under the shadow of Your wings, from the wicked who bring ruin to me, from my deadly enemies who surround me.

—Psalm 17:8–9

For strangers rise up against me, and formidable adversaries seek my life; they do not set God before them. Selah

—Psalm 54:3

For oppression brings confusion to the wise man, and a bribe destroys a man's heart.

—Ecclesiastes 7:7

In righteousness you shall be established; you shall be far from oppression, for you shall not fear, and from terror, for it shall not come near you.

—Isaiah 54:14

OVERWHELMED

Do not fret because of evildoers, nor be jealous of those who do injustice. For they will quickly wither like the grass, and fade like the green herbs. Trust in the Lord, and do good; dwell in the land, and practice faithfulness. Delight yourself in the Lord, and He will give you the desires of your heart.

—Psalm 37:1–4

But Jesus looked at them and said, "With men this is impossible, but with God all things are possible."

—Matthew 19:26

But when the Spirit of truth comes, He will guide you into all truth. For He will not speak on His own authority. But He will speak whatever He hears, and He will tell you things that are to come.

—John 16:13

But He said to me, "My grace is sufficient for you, for My strength is made perfect in weakness." Therefore most gladly I will boast in my weaknesses, that the power of Christ may rest upon me.

—2 Corinthians 12:9

But my God shall supply your every need according to His riches in glory by Christ Jesus.

—Philippians 4:19

PATIENCE

Rest in the Lord, and wait patiently for Him; do not fret because of those who prosper in their way, because of those who make wicked schemes.

—Psalm 37:7

But he who endures to the end shall be saved.

—Matthew 24:13

Not only so, but we also boast in tribulation, knowing that tribulation produces patience, patience produces character, and character produces hope.

—Romans 5:3–4

137

Love suffers long and is kind; love envies not; love flaunts not itself and is not puffed up, does not behave itself improperly, seeks not its own, is not easily provoked, thinks no evil.

—1 Corinthians 13:4–5

And let us not grow weary in doing good, for in due season we shall reap, if we do not give up.

—Galatians 6:9

Now we exhort you, brothers, warn those who are unruly, comfort the faint-hearted, support the weak, and be patient toward everyone. See that no one renders evil for evil to anyone. But always seek to do good to one another and to all.

—1 Thessalonians 5:14–15

PEACE

The Lord will give strength to His people; the Lord will bless His people with peace.

—Psalm 29:11

When a man's ways please the Lord, He makes even his enemies to be at peace with him.

—Proverbs 16:7

You will keep him in perfect peace, whose mind is stayed on You, because he trusts in You.

—Isaiah 26:3

Peace I leave with you. My peace I give to you. Not as the world gives do I give to you. Let not your heart be troubled, neither let it be afraid.

—John 14:27

Now may the God of hope fill you with all joy and peace in believing, so that you may abound in hope, through the power of the Holy Spirit.

—Romans 15:13

And the peace of God, which surpasses all understanding, will protect your hearts and minds through Christ Jesus.

—Philippians 4:7

PEER PRESSURE

Blessed is the man who walks not in the counsel of the ungodly, nor stands in the path of sinners, nor sits in the seat of scoffers; but his delight is in the law of the Lord, and in His law he meditates day and night.

—Psalm 1:1–2

He who walks with wise men will be wise, but a companion of fools will be destroyed.

—Proverbs 13:20

No temptation has taken you except what is common to man. God is faithful, and He will not permit you to be tempted above what you can endure, but will with the temptation also make a way to escape, that you may be able to bear it.

—1 Corinthians 10:13

For am I now seeking the approval of men or of God? Or am I trying to please men? For if I were still trying to please men, I would not be the servant of Christ.

—Galatians 1:10

Blessed is the man who endures temptation, for when he is tried, he will receive the crown of life, which the Lord has promised to those who love Him. Let no man say when he is tempted, "I am tempted by God," for God cannot be tempted with evil; neither does He tempt anyone. But each man is tempted when he is drawn away by his own lust and enticed. Then, when lust has conceived, it brings forth sin; and when sin is finished, it brings forth death.

—James 1:12–15

PERSEVERANCE IN ADVERSITY

And call on Me in the day of trouble; I will deliver you, and you will glorify Me.

—Psalm 50:15

When you pass through waters, I will be with you. And through the rivers, they shall not overflow you. When you walk through the fire, you shall not be burned, nor shall the flame kindle on you.

—Isaiah 43:2

Not only so, but we also boast in tribulation, knowing that tribulation produces patience, patience produces character, and character produces hope. And hope does not disappoint, because the love of God is shed abroad in our hearts by the Holy Spirit who has been given to us.

—Romans 5:3–5

For I consider that the sufferings of this present time are not worthy to be compared with the glory which shall be revealed to us.

—Romans 8:18

My brothers, count it all joy when you fall into diverse temptations, knowing that the trying of your faith develops patience. But let patience perfect its work, that you may be perfect and complete, lacking nothing.

—James 1:2–4

PERSPECTIVE

But the Lord said to Samuel, "Do not look on his appearance or on the height of his stature, because I have rejected him. For the Lord sees not as man sees. For man looks on the outward appearance, but the Lord looks on the heart."

—1 Samuel 16:7

The counsel of the LORD stands forever, the purposes of His heart to all generations.

—PSALM 33:11

For My thoughts are not your thoughts, nor are your ways My ways, says the LORD. For as the heavens are higher than the earth, so are My ways higher than your ways, and My thoughts than your thoughts.

—ISAIAH 55:8–9

Teaching them to observe all things I have commanded you. And remember, I am with you always, even to the end of the age.

—MATTHEW 28:20

O the depth of the riches and wisdom and knowledge of God! How unsearchable are His judgments and unfathomable are His ways! "For who has known the mind of the Lord? Or who has become His counselor?" "Or who has first given to Him, and it shall be repaid to him?" For from Him and through Him and to Him are all things. To Him be glory forever! Amen.

—ROMANS 11:33–36

PORNOGRAPHY

But I say to you that whoever looks on a woman to lust after her has committed adultery with her already in his heart.

—MATTHEW 5:28

No temptation has taken you except what is common to man. God is faithful, and He will not permit you to be tempted above what you can endure, but will with the temptation also make a way to escape, that you may be able to bear it.

—1 Corinthians 10:13

Now the works of the flesh are revealed, which are these: adultery, sexual immorality, impurity, lewdness.

—Galatians 5:19

And do not have fellowship with the unfruitful works of darkness; instead, expose them. For it is shameful even to speak of those things which are done by them in secret.

—Ephesians 5:11–12

For all that is in the world—the lust of the flesh, the lust of the eyes, and the pride of life—is not of the Father, but is of the world.

—1 John 2:16

POSITION IN GOD

I am the true vine, and My Father is the vinedresser...I am the vine, you are the branches. He who remains in Me, and I in him, bears much fruit. For without Me you can do nothing.

—John 15:1–5

Do you not know that you are the temple of God, and that the Spirit of God dwells in you?

—1 Corinthians 3:16

Now, therefore, you are no longer strangers and foreigners, but are fellow citizens with the saints and members of the household of God.

—Ephesians 2:19

And that you put on the new nature, which was created according to God in righteousness and true holiness.

—Ephesians 4:24

Be sober and watchful, because your adversary the devil walks around as a roaring lion, seeking whom he may devour.

—1 Peter 5:8

POVERTY

For the Lord hears the poor, and does not despise His prisoners.

—Psalm 69:33

Indeed, may he deliver the needy when he cries; the poor also, and him who has no helper. May he have compassion on the poor and needy, and save the lives of the needy.

—Psalm 72:12–13

He will regard the prayer of the destitute and will not despise their prayer.

—Psalm 102:17

Yet He raises up the poor from affliction and cares for their families like flocks of sheep.

—Psalm 107:41

He raises up the poor out of the dust and lifts the needy out of the ash heap.

—Psalm 113:7

I will abundantly bless her provisions; I will satisfy her poor with bread.

—Psalm 132:15

Sing to the Lord, praise the Lord. For He has delivered the soul of the poor from the hand of evildoers.

—Jeremiah 20:13

POWER

O God, You are awesome from Your sanctuaries; the God of Israel is He who gives strength and power to people. Blessed be God!

—Psalm 68:35

Great is our Lord and great in power; His understanding is without measure.

—Psalm 147:5

A wise man is strong; yes, a man of knowledge increases strength.

—Proverbs 24:5

Behold, I am the Lord, the God of all flesh. Is anything too hard for Me?

—Jeremiah 32:27

And all the inhabitants of the earth are reputed as nothing; and He does according to His will in the army of heaven and among the inhabitants of the earth. And no one can stay His hand or say to Him, "What have You done?"

—Daniel 4:35

The Lord is slow to anger and great in power, and the Lord will in no way acquit the guilty. In gale winds and a storm is His way, and clouds are the dust of His feet.

—Nahum 1:3

POWER OF GOD'S WORD

My son, attend to my words; incline your ear to my sayings. Do not let them depart from your eyes; keep them in the midst of your heart; for they are life to those who find them, and health to all their body.

—Proverbs 4:20–22

Every word of God is pure; He is a shield to those who put their trust in Him.

—Proverbs 30:5

Heaven and earth will pass away, but My words will never pass away.

—Matthew 24:35

My speech and my preaching was not with enticing words of man's wisdom, but in demonstration of the Spirit and of power.

—1 Corinthians 2:4

For the word of God is alive, and active, and sharper than any two-edged sword, piercing even to the division of soul and spirit, of joints and marrow, and able to judge the thoughts and intents of the heart.

—Hebrews 4:12

POWER OF JESUS' NAME

Then Jesus came and spoke to them, saying, "All authority has been given to Me in heaven and on earth."

—Matthew 28:18

Look, I give you authority to trample on serpents and scorpions, and over all the power of the enemy. And nothing shall by any means hurt you.

—Luke 10:19

But these are written that you might believe that Jesus is the Christ, the Son of God, and that believing you may have life in His name.

—John 20:31

Then Peter said, "I have no silver and gold, but I give you what I have. In the name of Jesus Christ of Nazareth, rise up and walk."

—Acts 3:6

Now, Lord, look on their threats and grant that Your servants may speak Your word with great boldness, by stretching out Your hand to heal and that signs and wonders may be performed in the name of Your holy Son Jesus.

—Acts 4:29–30

POWER OF PRAISE

You alone are the Lord. You have made heaven, the heaven of heavens, with all their host, the earth and all that is on it, the seas and all that is in them; and You preserve them all. And the host of heaven worships You.

—Nehemiah 9:6

Shout joyfully to God, all you lands! Sing out the glory of His name; make His praise glorious. Say to God, "How awesome are Your works! Through the greatness of Your power Your enemies cringe before You. All the earth will worship You and will sing to You; they will sing to Your name." Selah

—Psalm 66:1–4

O come, let us worship and bow down; let us kneel before the Lord, our Maker. For He is our God, and we are the people of His pasture and the sheep of His hand.

—Psalm 95:6–7

I will greatly praise the Lord with my mouth; indeed, I will praise Him among the multitude. For He stands at the right hand of the poor, to save him from those who condemn his soul to death.

—Psalm 109:30–31

Without question, great is the mystery of godliness: God was revealed in the flesh, justified in the Spirit, seen by angels, preached to the Gentiles, believed on in the world, taken up into glory.

—1 Timothy 3:16

Through Him, then, let us continually offer to God the sacrifice of praise, which is the fruit of our lips, giving thanks to His name.

—Hebrews 13:15

POWER OF THE TONGUE

In the multitude of words sin is not lacking, but he who restrains his lips is wise.

—Proverbs 10:19

A soft answer turns away wrath, but grievous words stir up anger.

—Proverbs 15:1

Death and life are in the power of the tongue, and those who love it will eat its fruit.

—Proverbs 18:21

Let no unwholesome word proceed out of your mouth, but only that which is good for building up, that it may give grace to the listeners.

—Ephesians 4:29

If anyone among you seems to be religious and does not bridle his tongue, but deceives his own heart, this man's religion is vain.

—James 1:26

PRAYER

He shall call upon Me, and I will answer him; I will be with him in trouble, and I will deliver him and honor him.

—Psalm 91:15

The sacrifice of the wicked is an abomination to the Lord, but the prayer of the upright is His delight.

—Proverbs 15:8

The Lord is far from the wicked, but He hears the prayer of the righteous.

—Proverbs 15:29

But you, when you pray, enter your closet, and when you have shut your door, pray to your Father who is in secret. And your Father who sees in secret will reward you openly.

—Matthew 6:6

Again I say to you, that if two of you agree on earth about anything they ask, it will be done for them by My Father who is in heaven. For where two or three are assembled in My name, there I am in their midst.

—Matthew 18:19–20

PRAYING WITH POWER

Ask and it will be given to you; seek and you will find; knock and it will be opened to you. For everyone who asks receives, and he who seeks finds, and to him who knocks, it will be opened. What man is there among you who, if his son asks for bread, will give him a stone? Or if he asks for a fish, will he give him a snake? If you then, being evil, know how to give good gifts to your children, how much more will your Father who is in heaven give good things to those who ask Him!

—Matthew 7:7–11

Likewise, the Spirit helps us in our weaknesses, for we do not know what to pray for as we ought, but the Spirit Himself intercedes for us with groanings too deep for words.

—Romans 8:26

You ask, and do not receive, because you ask amiss, that you may spend it on your passions.

—James 4:3

151

And the prayer of faith will save the sick, and the Lord will raise him up. And if he has committed any sins, he will be forgiven.

—James 5:15

Confess your faults to one another and pray for one another, that you may be healed. The effective, fervent prayer of a righteous man accomplishes much.

—James 5:16

PRIDE

When pride comes, then comes shame; but with the humble is wisdom.

—Proverbs 11:2

Only by pride comes contention, but with the well-advised is wisdom.

—Proverbs 13:10

Everyone who is proud in heart is an abomination to the Lord; be assured, he will not be unpunished.

—Proverbs 16:5

Pride goes before destruction, and a haughty spirit before a fall.

—Proverbs 16:18

He who is of a proud heart stirs up strife, but he who puts his trust in the LORD will prosper. He who trusts in his own heart is a fool, but whoever walks wisely will be delivered.

—Proverbs 28:25–26

A man's pride will bring him low, but honor will uphold the humble in spirit.

—Proverbs 29:23

PRIORITIES

I have set the LORD always before me; because He is at my right hand, I will not be moved. Therefore my heart is glad, and my glory rejoices; my flesh also will rest in security. For You will not leave my soul in Sheol, nor will You suffer Your godly one to see corruption. You will make known to me the path of life; in Your presence is fullness of joy; at Your right hand there are pleasures for evermore.

—Psalm 16:8–11

He who follows after righteousness and mercy finds life, righteousness, and honor.

—Proverbs 21:21

Prepare your work outside, and make it fit for yourself in the field; and afterwards build your house.

—Proverbs 24:27

For what does it profit a man if he gains the whole world and loses his own soul? Or what will a man give in exchange for his soul?

—Mark 8:36–37

For where your treasure is, there will your heart be also.

—Luke 12:34

PROSPEROUS

But you must remember the Lord your God, for it is He who gives you the ability to get wealth, so that He may establish His covenant which He swore to your fathers, as it is today.

—Deuteronomy 8:18

For you shall eat the fruit of the labor of your hands; you will be happy, and it shall be well with you.

—Psalm 128:2

The blessing of the Lord makes rich, and He adds no sorrow with it.

—Proverbs 10:22

He who is of a proud heart stirs up strife, but he who puts his trust in the Lord will prosper.

—Proverbs 28:25

Bring all the tithes into the storehouse, that there may be food in My house, and test Me now in this, says the Lord of Hosts, if I will not open for you the windows of heaven and pour out for you a blessing, that there will not be room enough to receive it.

—MALACHI 3:10

PROTECTION

For the eyes of the LORD move about on all the earth to strengthen the heart that is completely toward Him. You have acted foolishly in this, and from this point forward you will have wars.

—2 CHRONICLES 16:9

He shall not be afraid of evil tidings; his heart is fixed, trusting in the LORD.

—PSALM 112:7

But whoever listens to me will dwell safely, and will be secure from fear of evil.

—PROVERBS 1:33

When you lie down, you will not be afraid; yes, you will lie down and your sleep will be sweet.

—PROVERBS 3:24

The name of the LORD is a strong tower; the righteous run into it and are safe.

—PROVERBS 18:10

But now, thus says the LORD who created you, O Jacob, and He who formed you, O Israel: Do not fear, for I have redeemed

155

you; I have called you by your name; you are Mine. When you pass through waters, I will be with you. And through the rivers, they shall not overflow you. When you walk through the fire, you shall not be burned, nor shall the flame kindle on you.

—Isaiah 43:1–2

PROVISION

Now it will be, if you will diligently obey the voice of the Lord your God, being careful to do all His commandments which I am commanding you today, then the Lord your God will set you high above all the nations of the earth. And all these blessings will come on you and overtake you if you listen to the voice of the Lord your God.

—Deuteronomy 28:1–2

I have been young, and now am old; yet I have not seen the righteous forsaken, nor their offspring begging bread. The righteous are gracious and lend, and their offspring are a source of blessing.

—Psalm 37:25–26

God is able to make all grace abound toward you, so that you, always having enough of everything, may abound to every good work.

—2 Corinthians 9:8

I do not speak because I have need, for I have learned in whatever state I am to be content. I know both how to face humble circumstances and how to have abundance. Everywhere and in all things I have learned the secret, both to be full and to be hungry, both to abound and to suffer need.

—Philippians 4:11–12

But my God shall supply your every need according to His riches in glory by Christ Jesus.

—Philippians 4:19

PUNISHMENT

My son, do not despise the chastening of the Lord, nor be weary of His correction; for whom the Lord loves He corrects, even as a father the son in whom he delights.

—Proverbs 3:11–12

Your own wickedness will correct you, and your backslidings will reprove you. Know therefore and see that it is an evil thing and bitter for you to have forsaken the Lord your God, and the fear of Me is not in you, says the Lord God of Hosts.

—Jeremiah 2:19

But he who does wrong will receive for the wrong which he has done, and there is no partiality.

—Colossians 3:25

For God has not appointed us to wrath, but to obtain salvation by our Lord Jesus Christ, who died for us, so that whether we are awake or asleep, we should live together with Him.

—1 Thessalonians 5:9–10

And to give you who are troubled rest with us when the Lord Jesus is revealed from heaven with His mighty angels, in flaming fire taking vengeance on those who do not know God and do not obey the gospel of our Lord Jesus Christ.

—2 Thessalonians 1:7–8

For if the word spoken by angels was true, and every sin and disobedience received a just recompense, how shall we escape if we neglect such a great salvation, which was first declared by the Lord, and was confirmed to us by those who heard Him?

—Hebrews 2:2–3

PURITY

How shall a young man keep his way pure? By keeping it according to Your word.

—Psalm 119:9

Blessed are the pure in heart, for they shall see God.

—Matthew 5:8

Escape from sexual immorality. Every sin that a man commits is outside the body. But he who commits sexual immorality sins against his own body.

—1 Corinthians 6:18

For this you know, that no sexually immoral or impure person, or one who is greedy, who is an idolater, has any inheritance in the kingdom of Christ and of God.

—Ephesians 5:5

For this is the will of God, your sanctification: that you should abstain from sexual immorality, that each one of you should know how to possess his own vessel in sanctification and honor, not in the lust of depravity, even as the Gentiles who do not know God.

—1 Thessalonians 4:3–5

Let no one despise your youth, but be an example to the believers in speech, in conduct, in love, in spirit, in faith, and in purity.

—1 Timothy 4:12

PURPOSE

The Lord will fulfill His purpose for me; Your mercy, O Lord, endures forever. Do not forsake the works of Your hands.

—Psalm 138:8

The Lord has made all things for Himself, yes, even the wicked for the day of evil.

—Proverbs 16:4

For I know the plans that I have for you, says the Lord, plans for peace and not for evil, to give you a future and a hope.

—Jeremiah 29:11

We know that all things work together for good to those who love God, to those who are called according to His purpose.

—Romans 8:28

For we are His workmanship, created in Christ Jesus for good works, which God prepared beforehand, so that we should walk in them.

—Ephesians 2:10

REBELLION

God sets the deserted in families; He brings out prisoners into prosperity, but the rebellious dwell in a dry land.

—Psalm 68:6

But they rebelled and grieved His Holy Spirit; therefore, He turned Himself to be their enemy, and He fought against them.

—Isaiah 63:10

Beloved, do not avenge yourselves, but rather give place to God's wrath, for it is written: "Vengeance is Mine. I will repay," says the Lord.

—Romans 12:19

Follow the pattern of sound teaching which you have heard from me in the faith and love that is in Christ Jesus.

—2 Timothy 1:13

The Lord is not slow concerning His promise, as some count slowness. But He is patient with us, because He does not want any to perish, but all to come to repentance.

—2 Peter 3:9

REJECTION

The righteous cry out, and the Lord hears, and delivers them out of all their troubles. The Lord is near to the brokenhearted, and saves the contrite of spirit. Many are the afflictions of the righteous, but the Lord delivers him out of them all. A righteous one keeps all his bones; not one of them is broken.

—Psalm 34:17–20

For the Lord will not forsake His people; neither will He abandon His inheritance.

—Psalm 94:14

If the world hates you, you know that it hated Me before it hated you.

—John 15:18

But He said to me, "My grace is sufficient for you, for My strength is made perfect in weakness." Therefore most gladly I will boast in my weaknesses, that the power of Christ may rest upon me.

—2 Corinthians 12:9

Cast all your care upon Him, because He cares for you.

—1 Peter 5:7

RELATIONSHIPS

He who walks with wise men will be wise, but a companion of fools will be destroyed.

—Proverbs 13:20

A man who has friends must show himself friendly, and there is a friend who sticks closer than a brother.

—Proverbs 18:24

Iron sharpens iron, so a man sharpens the countenance of his friend.

—Proverbs 27:17

Two are better than one, because there is a good reward for their labor together. For if they fall, then one will help up his companion. But woe to him who is alone when he falls and has no one to help him up.…And if someone might overpower another by himself, two together can withstand him. A threefold cord is not quickly broken.

—Ecclesiastes 4:9–12

It shall not be so among you. Whoever would be great among you, let him serve you, and whoever would be first among you, let him be your slave, even as the Son of Man did not come to be served, but to serve and to give His life as a ransom for many.

—Matthew 20:26–28

For I say, through the grace given to me, to everyone among you, not to think of himself more highly than he ought to think, but to think with sound judgment, according to the measure of faith God has distributed to every man. For just as we have many parts in one body, and not all parts have the same function, so we, being many, are one body in Christ, and all are parts of one another.

—Romans 12:3–5

REPENTANCE

If My people, who are called by My name, will humble themselves and pray, and seek My face and turn from their wicked ways, then I will hear from heaven, and will forgive their sin and will heal their land.

—2 Chronicles 7:14

The Lord is near to the broken-hearted, and saves the contrite of spirit.

—Psalm 34:18

But if the wicked turns from all his sins that he has committed, and keeps all My statutes, and does that which is lawful and right, he shall surely live. He shall not die. All his transgressions that he has committed, they shall not be remembered against him. Because of his righteousness that he has done, he shall live.

—Ezekiel 18:21–22

But go and learn what this means, "I desire mercy, and not sacrifice." For I have not come to call the righteous, but sinners, to repentance.

—Matthew 9:13

Peter said to them, "Repent and be baptized, every one of you, in the name of Jesus Christ for the forgiveness of sins, and you shall receive the gift of the Holy Spirit."

—Acts 2:38

RESPECT

Honor your father and your mother, that your days may be long in the land which the Lord your God is giving you.

—Exodus 20:12

You shall rise up before a gray head, and honor the face of an old man, and fear your God: I am the Lord.

—Leviticus 19:32

Therefore, everything you would like men to do to you, do also to them, for this is the Law and the Prophets.

—Matthew 7:12

All men should honor the Son, just as they honor the Father. He who does not honor the Son does not honor the Father who sent Him.

—John 5:23

Be devoted to one another with brotherly love; prefer one another in honor.

—Romans 12:10

Honor all people. Love the brotherhood. Fear God. Honor the king.

—1 Peter 2:17

REST

And He said, "My presence will go with you, and I will give you rest."

—Exodus 33:14

Of Benjamin he said, "The beloved of the Lord will dwell in safety by Him, and the Lord will protect him all day long. He will dwell between His shoulders."

—Deuteronomy 33:12

He makes me lie down in green pastures; He leads me beside still waters. He restores my soul; He leads me in paths of righteousness for His name's sake.

—Psalm 23:2–3

It is in vain for you to rise up early, to stay up late, and to eat the bread of hard toil, for He gives sleep to His beloved.

—Psalm 127:2

He gives power to the faint, and to those who have no might He increases strength. Even the youths shall faint and be weary, and the young men shall utterly fall, but those who wait upon the Lord shall renew their strength; they shall mount up with wings as eagles, they shall run and not be weary, and they shall walk and not faint.

—Isaiah 40:29–31

REVENGE

You have heard that it was said, "An eye for an eye, and a tooth for a tooth." But I say to you, do not resist an evil person. But whoever strikes you on your right cheek, turn to him the other as well. And if anyone sues you in a court of law and takes away your tunic, let him have your cloak also. And whoever compels you to go a mile, go with him two.

—Matthew 5:38–41

For if you forgive men for their sins, your heavenly Father will also forgive you.

—Matthew 6:14

Beloved, do not avenge yourselves, but rather give place to God's wrath, for it is written: "Vengeance is Mine. I will repay," says the Lord.

—Romans 12:19

See that no one renders evil for evil to anyone. But always seek to do good to one another and to all.

—1 Thessalonians 5:15

For we know Him who said, "Vengeance is Mine," says the Lord, "I will repay." And again He says, "The Lord will judge His people." It is a fearful thing to fall into the hands of the living God.

—Hebrews 10:30–31

RIGHTEOUS LIVING

Blessed is the man who walks not in the counsel of the ungodly, nor stands in the path of sinners, nor sits in the seat of scoffers; but his delight is in the law of the Lord, and in His law he meditates day and night.

—Psalm 1:1–2

Surely goodness and mercy shall follow me all the days of my life, and I will dwell in the house of the Lord forever.

—Psalm 23:6

But seek first the kingdom of God and His righteousness, and all these things shall be given to you.

—Matthew 6:33

I am confident of this very thing, that He who began a good work in you will perfect it until the day of Jesus Christ.

—Philippians 1:6

If you then were raised with Christ, desire those things which are above, where Christ sits at the right hand of God. Set your affection on things above, not on things on earth.

—Colossians 3:1–2

Study to show yourself approved by God, a workman who need not be ashamed, rightly dividing the word of truth.

—2 TIMOTHY 2:15

ROLE MODELS

Hear, you children, the instruction of a father, and attend to know understanding.

—PROVERBS 4:1

My son, keep my words, and lay up my commandments within you. Keep my commandments and live, and my teaching as the apple of your eye. Bind them on your fingers, write them on the tablet of your heart.

—PROVERBS 7:1–3

Jesus said to him, "I am the way, the truth, and the life. No one comes to the Father except through Me."

—JOHN 14:6

In all things presenting yourself as an example of good works: in doctrine showing integrity, gravity, incorruptibility, and sound speech that cannot be condemned, so that the one who opposes you may be ashamed, having nothing evil to say of you.

—TITUS 2:7–8

For to this you were called, because Christ suffered for us, leaving us an example, that you should follow His steps.

—1 PETER 2:21

SATISFACTION

With long life I will satisfy him and show him My salvation.

—Psalm 91:16

Bless the Lord, O my soul, and all that is within me, bless His holy name. Bless the Lord, O my soul, and forget not all His benefits, who forgives all your iniquities, who heals all your diseases, who redeems your life from the pit, who crowns you with lovingkindness and tender mercies, who satisfies your mouth with good things, so that your youth is renewed like the eagle's.

—Psalm 103:1–5

And the Lord shall guide you continually, and satisfy your soul in drought, and strengthen your bones; and you shall be like a watered garden, and like a spring of water, whose waters do not fail.

—Isaiah 58:11

Jesus said to them, "I am the bread of life. Whoever comes to Me shall never hunger, and whoever believes in Me shall never thirst."

—John 6:35

In Him we have redemption through His blood and the forgiveness of sins according to the riches of His grace.

—Ephesians 1:7

Now faith is the substance of things hoped for, the evidence of things not seen.

—HEBREWS 11:1

SEEKING GOD

I love those who love me, and those who seek me early will find me.

—PROVERBS 8:17

You shall seek Me and find Me, when you shall search for Me with all your heart. I will be found by you, says the LORD, and I will turn away your captivity and gather you from all the nations and from all the places where I have driven you, says the LORD, and I will bring you back into the place from where I caused you to be carried away captive.

—JEREMIAH 29:13–14

The LORD is good to those who wait for Him, to the soul that seeks Him.

—LAMENTATIONS 3:25

Sow to yourselves righteousness, reap mercy, break up your fallow ground; for it is time to seek the LORD, until He comes and rains righteousness upon you.

—HOSEA 10:12

Indeed, thus says the LORD to the house of Israel: Seek Me and live!

—AMOS 5:4

SELF-CONTROL

A fool utters all his mind, but a wise man keeps it in until afterwards.

—Proverbs 29:11

But I bring and keep my body under subjection, lest when preaching to others I myself should be disqualified.

—1 Corinthians 9:27

But refuse profane and foolish myths. Instead, exercise in the ways of godliness. For bodily exercise profits a little, but godliness is profitable in all things, holding promise for the present life and also for the life to come.

—1 Timothy 4:7–8

Blessed is the man who endures temptation, for when he is tried, he will receive the crown of life, which the Lord has promised to those who love Him.

—James 1:12

For this reason make every effort to add virtue to your faith; and to your virtue, knowledge; and to your knowledge, self-control; and to your self-control, patient endurance; and to your patient endurance, godliness; and to your godliness, brotherly kindness; and to your brotherly kindness, love. For if these things reside in you and abound, they ensure that you will neither be useless nor unfruitful in the knowledge of our Lord Jesus Christ.

—2 Peter 1:5–8

SELF-DENIAL

But I say to you, do not resist an evil person. But whoever strikes you on your right cheek, turn to him the other as well. And if anyone sues you in a court of law and takes away your tunic, let him have your cloak also. And whoever compels you to go a mile, go with him two.

—Matthew 5:39–41

Then Jesus said to His disciples, "If anyone will come after Me, let him deny himself, and take up his cross, and follow Me. For whoever would save his life will lose it, and whoever loses his life for My sake will find it. For what will it profit a man if he gains the whole world and loses his own soul? Or what shall a man give in exchange for his soul?"

—Matthew 16:24–26

Then He said to them all, "If anyone will come after Me, let him deny himself, and take up his cross daily, and follow Me. For whoever will save his life will lose it, but whoever loses his life for My sake will save it."

—Luke 9:23–24

He said to them, "Truly, I tell you, there is no man who has left his home or parents or brothers or wife or children, for the sake of the kingdom of God, who shall not receive many times more in this age and, in the age to come, eternal life."

—Luke 18:29–30

Therefore, brothers, we are debtors not to the flesh, to live according to the flesh. For if you live according to the flesh, you will die, but if through the Spirit you put to death the deeds of the body, you will live.

—Romans 8:12–13

SELF-ESTEEM

So God created man in His own image; in the image of God He created him; male and female He created them.

—Genesis 1:27

You brought my inner parts into being; You wove me in my mother's womb. I will praise you, for You made me with fear and wonder; marvelous are Your works, and You know me completely.

—Psalm 139:13–14

Therefore do not throw away your confidence, which will be greatly rewarded. For you need patience, so that after you have done the will of God, you will receive the promise.

—Hebrews 10:35–36

For I say, through the grace given to me, to everyone among you, not to think of himself more highly than he ought to think, but to think with sound judgment, according to the measure of faith God has distributed to every man.

—ROMANS 12:3

Do not let your adorning be the outward adorning of braiding the hair, wearing gold, or putting on fine clothing. But let it be the hidden nature of the heart, that which is not corruptible, even the ornament of a gentle and quiet spirit, which is very precious in the sight of God.

—1 PETER 3:3–4

SELF-IMAGE

Then God said, "Let us make man in our image, after our likeness, and let them have dominion over the fish of the sea, and over the birds of the air, and over the livestock, and over all the earth, and over every creeping thing that creeps on the earth." So God created man in His own image; in the image of God He created him; male and female He created them.

—GENESIS 1:26–27

For the LORD will be your confidence, and will keep your foot from being caught.

—PROVERBS 3:26

For as he thinks in his heart, so is he.

—PROVERBS 23:7

I am the vine, you are the branches. He who remains in Me, and I in him, bears much fruit. For without Me you can do nothing.

—John 15:5

For those whom He foreknew, He predestined to be conformed to the image of His Son, so that He might be the firstborn among many brothers.

—Romans 8:29

For we are His workmanship, created in Christ Jesus for good works, which God prepared beforehand, so that we should walk in them.

—Ephesians 2:10

SELF-RIGHTEOUSNESS

But we all are as an unclean thing, and all our righteousness is as filthy rags; and we all fade as a leaf, and our iniquities, like the wind, have taken us away.

—Isaiah 64:6

Yet you say, "Because I am innocent, surely His anger shall turn away from me." Now I will plead with you, because you say, "I have not sinned."

—Jeremiah 2:35

He said to them, "You are those who justify yourselves before men, but God knows your hearts. For that which is highly esteemed before men is an abomination before God."

—Luke 16:15

Jesus said, "If you were blind, you would have no sin. But now you say, 'We see.' Therefore your sin remains."

—John 9:41

But, "Let him who boasts, boast in the Lord." For it is not he who commends himself who is approved, but he whom the Lord commends.

—2 Corinthians 10:17–18

SELF-WORTH

What is man that You are mindful of him, or his descendants that You attend to them? For You have made him a little lower than God, and crowned him with glory and honor. You grant him dominion over the works of Your hands; You have put all things under his feet.

—Psalm 8:4–6

Better is the poor who walks in his uprightness, than he who is perverse in his ways, though he be rich.

—Proverbs 28:6

Before I formed you in the womb I knew you; and before you were born I sanctified you, and I ordained you a prophet to the nations.

—Jeremiah 1:5

Are not five sparrows sold for two pennies? Yet not one of them is forgotten by God. Indeed, even the hairs of your head are all numbered. Therefore do not fear. You are more valuable than many sparrows.

—Luke 12:6–7

For we are His workmanship, created in Christ Jesus for good works, which God prepared beforehand, so that we should walk in them.

—Ephesians 2:10

That He would give you, according to the riches of His glory, power to be strengthened by His Spirit in the inner man, and that Christ may dwell in your hearts through faith; that you, being rooted and grounded in love, may be able to comprehend with all saints what is the breadth and length and depth and height, and to know the love of Christ which surpasses knowledge; that you may be filled with all the fullness of God.

—Ephesians 3:16–19

SERVANTHOOD

You must follow after the LORD your God, fear Him, and keep His commandments, obey His voice, and you must serve Him, and cling to Him.

—DEUTERONOMY 13:4

Only carefully obey the commandment and the law that Moses the servant of the LORD commanded you: to love the LORD your God, to walk in all His ways, to obey His commandments, to cling to Him, and to serve Him with all your heart and soul.

—JOSHUA 22:5

If it is displeasing to you to serve the LORD, then choose today whom you will serve, if it should be the gods your fathers served beyond the River or the gods of the Amorites' land where you are now living. Yet as for me and my house, we will serve the LORD.

—JOSHUA 24:15

Fear the LORD: serve Him in truth with all your heart, and consider what great things He has done for you.

—1 SAMUEL 12:24

For whoever would save his life will lose it, and whoever loses his life for My sake will find it.

—MATTHEW 16:25

I urge you therefore, brothers, by the mercies of God, that you present your bodies as a living sacrifice, holy, and acceptable to God, which is your reasonable service of worship

—Romans 12:1

SHAME

O my God, I trust in You; may I not be ashamed; may my enemies not triumph over me. Yes, let none who wait on You be ashamed; let them be ashamed who transgress without cause.

—Psalm 25:2–3

Let my heart be blameless in Your statutes, that I may not be ashamed.

—Psalm 119:80

But he was wounded for our transgressions, he was bruised for our iniquities; the chastisement of our peace was upon him, and by his stripes we are healed.

—Isaiah 53:5

Do not fear, for you shall not be ashamed nor be humiliated; for you shall not be put to shame, for you shall forget the shame of your youth and shall not remember the reproach of your widowhood anymore. For your Maker is your husband. The Lord of Hosts is His name. And your Redeemer is the Holy One of Israel. He shall be called the God of the whole earth.

—Isaiah 54:4–5

For the Scripture says, "Whoever believes in Him will not be ashamed."

—Romans 10:11

SPIRITUAL GROWTH

Blessed is the man who walks not in the counsel of the ungodly, nor stands in the path of sinners, nor sits in the seat of scoffers; but his delight is in the law of the LORD, and in His law he meditates day and night. He will be like a tree planted by the rivers of water, that brings forth its fruit in its season; its leaf will not wither, and whatever he does will prosper.

—Psalm 1:1–3

But whoever drinks of the water that I shall give him will never thirst. Indeed, the water that I shall give him will become in him a well of water springing up into eternal life.

—John 4:14

But, speaking the truth in love, we may grow up in all things into Him, who is the head, Christ Himself, from whom the whole body is joined together and connected by every joint and ligament, as every part effectively does its work and grows, building itself up in love.

—Ephesians 4:15–16

For this reason we also, since the day we heard it, do not cease to pray for you and to ask that you may be filled with the knowledge of His will in all wisdom and spiritual understanding;

that you may walk in a manner worthy of the Lord, pleasing to all, being fruitful in every good work, and increasing in the knowledge of God.

—Colossians 1:9–10

But grow in the grace and knowledge of our Lord and Savior Jesus Christ. To Him be glory, both now and forever. Amen.

—2 Peter 3:18

STABILITY

He also brought me up out of a horrible pit, out of the miry clay, and set my feet on a rock, and established my steps.

—Psalm 40:2

He who walks uprightly walks surely, but he who perverts his ways will be known.

—Proverbs 10:9

The wicked flee when no man pursues, but the righteous are bold as a lion. Because of the transgression of a land, many are its princes; but by a man of understanding and knowledge, it shall be prolonged.

—Proverbs 28:1–2

Therefore we should be more attentive to what we have heard, lest we drift away.

—Hebrews 2:1

Therefore, since we are receiving a kingdom that cannot be moved, let us be gracious, by which we may serve God acceptably with reverence and godly fear.

—Hebrews 12:28

If any of you lacks wisdom, let him ask of God, who gives to all men liberally and without criticism, and it will be given to him. But let him ask in faith, without wavering. For he who wavers is like a wave of the sea, driven and tossed with the wind.

—James 1:5–6

STANDING AGAINST WORLDLINESS

If you were of the world, the world would love you as its own. But because you are not of the world, since I chose you out of the world, the world therefore hates you.

—John 15:19

Do not be conformed to this world, but be transformed by the renewing of your mind, that you may prove what is the good and acceptable and perfect will of God.

—Romans 12:2

Set your affection on things above, not on things on earth.

—Colossians 3:2

Teaching us that, denying ungodliness and worldly desires, we should live soberly, righteously, and in godliness in this present world.

—Titus 2:12

Do not love the world or the things in the world. If anyone loves the world, the love of the Father is not in him. For all that is in the world—the lust of the flesh, the lust of the eyes, and the pride of life—is not of the Father, but is of the world. The world and its desires are passing away, but the one who does the will of God lives forever.

—1 John 2:15–17

STRENGTH

O God, You are awesome from Your sanctuaries; the God of Israel is He who gives strength and power to people. Blessed be God!

—Psalm 68:35

He gives power to the faint, and to those who have no might He increases strength.

—Isaiah 40:29

But those who wait upon the Lord shall renew their strength; they shall mount up with wings as eagles, they shall run and not be weary, and they shall walk and not faint.

—Isaiah 40:31

Do not fear, for I am with you; do not be dismayed, for I am your God. I will strengthen you, I will help you, yes, I will uphold you with My righteous right hand.

—Isaiah 41:10

But He said to me, "My grace is sufficient for you, for My strength is made perfect in weakness." Therefore most gladly I will boast in my weaknesses, that the power of Christ may rest upon me. So I take pleasure in weaknesses, in reproaches, in hardships, in persecutions, and in distresses for Christ's sake. For when I am weak, then I am strong.

—2 Corinthians 12:9–10

STRESS

Cast your burden on the Lord, and He will sustain you; He will never allow the righteous to be moved.

—Psalm 55:22

Except the Lord build the house, those who build labor in vain; except the Lord guards the city, the watchman stays awake in vain. It is in vain for you to rise up early, to stay up late, and to eat the bread of hard toil, for He gives sleep to His beloved.

—Psalm 127:1–2

Heaviness in the heart of man makes it droop, but a good word makes it glad.

—Proverbs 12:25

Come to Me, all you who labor and are heavily burdened, and I will give you rest. Take My yoke upon you, and learn from

Me. For I am meek and lowly in heart, and you will find rest for your souls. For My yoke is easy, and My burden is light.

—Matthew 11:28–30

Peace I leave with you. My peace I give to you. Not as the world gives do I give to you. Let not your heart be troubled, neither let it be afraid.

—John 14:27

SUCCESS

The Lord your God will make you prosper in every work of your hand, in the offspring of your body, and in the offspring of your livestock, and in the produce of your land, for good. For the Lord will once again rejoice over you for good, just as He rejoiced over your fathers.

—Deuteronomy 30:9

For you shall eat the fruit of the labor of your hands; you will be happy, and it shall be well with you.

—Psalm 128:2

And also everyone to whom God has given wealth and possessions, and given him power to enjoy them, and to receive his reward and to rejoice in his labor—this is the gift of God.

—Ecclesiastes 5:19

Then He shall give you rain for the seed which you shall sow in the ground and bread of the increase of the earth. And it shall be rich and plentiful. On that day your cattle shall feed in large pastures.

—Isaiah 30:23

His divine power has given to us all things that pertain to life and godliness through the knowledge of Him who has called us by His own glory and excellence.

—2 Peter 1:3

TAKING AWAY FEAR

Be strong and of a good courage. Fear not, nor be afraid of them, for the Lord your God, it is He who goes with you. He will not fail you, nor forsake you.

—Deuteronomy 31:6

The Lord is my light and my salvation; whom will I fear? The Lord is the strength of my life; of whom will I be afraid?

—Psalm 27:1

Do not be afraid of sudden terror, nor of trouble from the wicked when it comes. For the Lord will be your confidence, and will keep your foot from being caught.

—Proverbs 3:25–26

In the day the Lord gives you rest from your sorrow, and from your fear, and from the hard bondage in which you were made to serve.

—Isaiah 14:3

There is no fear in love, but perfect love casts out fear, because fear has to do with punishment. Whoever fears is not perfect in love.

—1 John 4:18

TALENTS

But you must remember the Lord your God, for it is He who gives you the ability to get wealth, so that He may establish His covenant which He swore to your fathers, as it is today.

—Deuteronomy 8:18

May He grant you according to your own heart, and fulfill all your counsel.

—Psalm 20:4

A man's gift makes room for him, and brings him before great men.

—Proverbs 18:16

For to a man who is pleasing before Him, God gives wisdom, knowledge, and joy; but to the sinner He gives the work of gathering and collecting to give him who is pleasing before God. Also this is vanity and chasing the wind.

—Ecclesiastes 2:26

For the gifts and calling of God are irrevocable.

—Romans 11:29

Let no one despise your youth, but be an example to the believers in speech, in conduct, in love, in spirit, in faith and in purity. Until I come, give attention to reading, exhortation, and doctrine. Do not neglect the gift that is in you, which was given to you by prophecy, with the laying on of hands by the elders.

—1 TIMOTHY 4:12–14

TEMPTATION

My son, if sinners entice you, do not consent.

—PROVERBS 1:10

Watch and pray that you enter not into temptation. The spirit indeed is willing, but the flesh is weak.

—MATTHEW 26:41

When He came there, He said to them, "Pray that you may not fall into temptation."

—LUKE 22:40

Put on the whole armor of God that you may be able to stand against the schemes of the devil. For our fight is not against flesh and blood, but against principalities, against powers, against the rulers of the darkness of this world, and against spiritual forces of evil in the heavenly places.

—EPHESIANS 6:11–12

For we do not have a High Priest who cannot sympathize with our weaknesses, but One who was in every sense tempted like we are, yet without sin.

—Hebrews 4:15

THANKFULNESS

Give thanks to the Lord, call on His name; make known His deeds among the peoples.

—1 Chronicles 16:8

The Lord is my strength and my shield; my heart trusted in Him, and I was helped; therefore my heart rejoices, and with my song I will thank Him.

—Psalm 28:7

Now thanks be to God who always causes us to triumph in Christ and through us reveals the fragrance of His knowledge in every place.

—2 Corinthians 2:14

Be anxious for nothing, but in everything, by prayer and supplication with gratitude, make your requests known to God.

—Philippians 4:6

In everything give thanks, for this is the will of God in Christ Jesus concerning you.

—1 Thessalonians 5:18

For everything created by God is good, and not to be refused if it is received with thanksgiving.

—1 Timothy 4:4

TRIALS

Not only so, but we also boast in tribulation, knowing that tribulation produces patience, patience produces character, and character produces hope. And hope does not disappoint, because the love of God is shed abroad in our hearts by the Holy Spirit who has been given to us.

—Romans 5:3–5

No temptation has taken you except what is common to man. God is faithful, and He will not permit you to be tempted above what you can endure, but will with the temptation also make a way to escape, that you may be able to bear it.

—1 Corinthians 10:13

My brothers, count it all joy when you fall into diverse temptations, knowing that the trying of your faith develops patience. But let patience perfect its work, that you may be perfect and complete, lacking nothing.

—James 1:2–4

Blessed is the man who endures temptation, for when he is tried, he will receive the crown of life, which the Lord has promised to those who love Him.

—James 1:12

Beloved, do not be surprised at the fiery ordeal that is taking place among you to test you, as though some strange thing happened to you. But rejoice in so far as you share in Christ's sufferings, so that you may rejoice and be glad also in the revelation of His glory.

—1 Peter 4:12–13

TROUBLE

For in the time of trouble He will hide me in His pavilion; in the shelter of His tabernacle He will hide me; He will set me up on a rock.

—Psalm 27:5

But the salvation of the righteous is from the Lord; He is their refuge in the time of distress. The Lord will help them and deliver them; He will deliver them from the wicked, and save them, because they take refuge in Him.

—Psalm 37:39–40

God is our refuge and strength, a well-proven help in trouble.

—Psalm 46:1

Cast your burden on the Lord, and He will sustain you; He will never allow the righteous to be moved.

—Psalm 55:22

Peace I leave with you. My peace I give to you. Not as the world gives do I give to you. Let not your heart be troubled, neither let it be afraid.

—John 14:27

Blessed be God, the Father of our Lord Jesus Christ, the Father of mercies, and the God of all comfort, 4 who comforts us in all our tribulation, that we may be able to comfort those who are in any trouble by the comfort with which we ourselves are comforted by God.

—2 Corinthians 1:3–4

TRUST

The God of my strength, in whom I will trust; My shield and the horn of my salvation, My fortress and my sanctuary; My Savior, You save me from violence.

—2 Samuel 22:3

He trusted in the Lord God of Israel. Afterwards, there was no one like him among all the kings of Judah or among those who were before him.

—2 Kings 18:5

Though He slay me, yet will I trust in Him, but I will defend my own ways before Him.

—Job 13:15

To You, O Lord, do I lift up my soul. O my God, I trust in You; may I not be ashamed; may my enemies not triumph over me. Yes, let none who wait on You be ashamed; let them be ashamed who transgress without cause.

—Psalm 25:1–3

Blessed is the man who places trust in the Lord, but does not turn toward the proud, nor those falling away to falsehood.

—Psalm 40:4

Those who trust in the Lord shall be as Mount Zion, which cannot be removed, but abides forever.

—Psalm 125:1

UNDERSTANDING

The giving of Your words gives light; it grants understanding to the simple.

—Psalm 119:130

He who is slow to wrath is of great understanding, but he who is hasty of spirit exalts folly.

—Proverbs 14:29

He who has knowledge spares his words, and a man of understanding is of an excellent spirit.

—Proverbs 17:27

A fool has no delight in understanding, but in expressing his own heart.

—Proverbs 18:2

Counsel in the heart of man is like deep water, but a man of understanding will draw it out.

—Proverbs 20:5

UNITY

Now may the God of perseverance and encouragement grant you to live in harmony with one another in accordance with Christ Jesus.

—Romans 15:5

Now I ask you, brothers, by the name of our Lord Jesus Christ, that you all speak in agreement and that there be no divisions among you. But be perfectly joined together in the same mind and in the same judgment.

—1 Corinthians 1:10

Finally, brothers, farewell. Be perfect, be of good comfort, be of one mind, and live in peace, and the God of love and peace will be with you.

—2 Corinthians 13:11

Then fulfill my joy and be like-minded, having the same love, being in unity with one mind.

—Philippians 2:2

Finally, be all of one mind, be loving toward one another, be gracious, and be kind.

—1 Peter 3:8

UNSELFISHNESS

Greater love has no man than this: that a man lay down his life for his friends.

—John 15:13

Be devoted to one another with brotherly love; prefer one another in honor.

—Romans 12:10

Let each of you look not only to your own interests, but also to the interests of others.

—Philippians 2:4

Command those who are rich in this world that they not be conceited, nor trust in uncertain riches, but in the living God, who richly gives us all things to enjoy. Command that they do good, that they be rich in good works, generous, willing to share, and laying up in store for themselves a good foundation for the coming age, so that they may take hold of eternal life.

—1 Timothy 6:17–19

Confess your faults to one another and pray for one another, that you may be healed. The effective, fervent prayer of a righteous man accomplishes much.

—James 5:16

VALUES

Therefore, everything you would like men to do to you, do also to them, for this is the Law and the Prophets.

—Matthew 7:12

Jesus said to him, "'You shall love the Lord your God with all your heart, and with all your soul, and with all your mind.' This is the first and great commandment. And the second is like it: 'You shall love your neighbor as yourself.' On these two commandments hang all the Law and the Prophets."

—Matthew 22:37–40

Not only so, but we also boast in tribulation, knowing that tribulation produces patience, patience produces character, and character produces hope.

—Romans 5:3–4

But the fruit of the Spirit is love, joy, peace, patience, gentleness, goodness, faith, meekness, and self-control; against such there is no law.

—Galatians 5:22–23

So embrace, as the elect of God, holy and beloved, a spirit of mercy, kindness, humbleness of mind, meekness, and long-suffering. Bear with one another and forgive one another. If anyone has a quarrel against anyone, even as Christ forgave you, so you must do. And above all these things, embrace love, which is the bond of perfection.

—Colossians 3:12–14

VICTORY

For the Lord your God is He that goes with you, to fight for you against your enemies, to save you.

—Deuteronomy 20:4

Through God we shall be valiant, for He shall tread down our enemies.

—Psalm 108:13

No temptation has taken you except what is common to man. God is faithful, and He will not permit you to be tempted above what you can endure, but will with the temptation also make a way to escape, that you may be able to bear it.

—1 Corinthians 10:13

But He said to me, "My grace is sufficient for you, for My strength is made perfect in weakness." Therefore most gladly I will boast in my weaknesses, that the power of Christ may rest upon me. So I take pleasure in weaknesses, in reproaches, in hardships, in persecutions, and in distresses for Christ's sake. For when I am weak, then I am strong.

—2 Corinthians 12:9–10

I can do all things because of Christ who strengthens me.

—Philippians 4:13

WALKING IN GOD'S WAYS

But this thing I commanded them, saying, "Obey My voice, and I will be your God, and you shall be My people. And walk in all the ways that I have commanded you, that it may be well with you."

—Jeremiah 7:23

Bring all the tithes into the storehouse, that there may be food in My house, and test Me now in this, says the Lord of Hosts, if I will not open for you the windows of heaven and pour out for you a blessing, that there will not be room enough to receive it.

—Malachi 3:10

Give, and it will be given to you: Good measure, pressed down, shaken together, and running over will men give unto you. For with the measure you use, it will be measured unto you.

—Luke 6:38

For you were formerly darkness, but now you are light in the Lord. Walk as children of light.

—Ephesians 5:8

See then that you walk carefully, not as fools, but as wise men.

—Ephesians 5:15

WEALTH

A good man leaves an inheritance to his children's children, and the wealth of the sinner is laid up for the just.

—PROVERBS 13:22

The rich rules over the poor, and the borrower is servant to the lender.

—PROVERBS 22:7

Do not store up for yourselves treasures on earth where moth and rust destroy and where thieves break in and steal. But store up for yourselves treasures in heaven, where neither moth nor rust destroy and where thieves do not break in nor steal, for where your treasure is, there will your heart be also.

—MATTHEW 6:19–21

No one can serve two masters. For either he will hate the one and love the other, or else he will hold to the one and despise the other. You cannot serve God and money.

—MATTHEW 6:24

For the love of money is the root of all evil. While coveting after money, some have strayed from the faith and pierced themselves through with many sorrows.

—1 TIMOTHY 6:10

WILL OF GOD

Make me to know Your ways, O Lord; teach me Your paths. Lead me in Your truth and teach me, for You are the God of my salvation; on You I wait all the day.

—Psalm 25:4–5

I will instruct you and teach you in the way you should go; I will counsel you with my eye on you. Do not be as the horse or as the mule that are without understanding, that must be restrained with bit and bridle, or they will not come near you.

—Psalm 32:8–9

I delight to do Your will, O my God; Your law is within my inward parts.

—Psalm 40:8

Your word is a lamp to my feet, and a light to my path.

—Psalm 119:105

Cause me to hear Your lovingkindness in the morning; for in You I have my trust; cause me to know the way I should walk, for I lift up my soul unto You.

—Psalm 143:8

WISDOM

From where then does wisdom come? And where is the place of understanding? It is hidden from the eyes of all living and concealed from the birds of the air.

—Job 28:20–21

To man He said: "Look, the fear of the Lord, that is wisdom; And to depart from evil is understanding."

—Job 28:28

I have taught you in the way of wisdom; I have led you in right paths. When you walk, your steps will not be hindered, and when you run, you will not stumble.

—Proverbs 4:11–12

Get wisdom! Get understanding! Do not forget it, nor turn away from the words of my mouth.... Wisdom is principal; therefore get wisdom. And with all your getting, get understanding.

—Proverbs 4:5–7

For to a man who is pleasing before Him, God gives wisdom, knowledge, and joy; but to the sinner He gives the work of gathering and collecting to give him who is pleasing before God. Also this is vanity and chasing the wind.

—Ecclesiastes 2:26

WITNESSING

Go therefore and make disciples of all nations, baptizing them in the name of the Father and of the Son and of the Holy Spirit, Teaching them to observe all things I have commanded you. And remember, I am with you always, even to the end of the age. Amen.

—Matthew 28:19–20

He said to them, "Go into all the world, and preach the gospel to every creature. He who believes and is baptized will be saved. But he who does not believe will be condemned."

—Mark 16:15–16

Yet to all who received Him, He gave the power to become sons of God, to those who believed in His name.

—John 1:12

For I am not ashamed of the gospel of Christ. For it is the power of God for salvation to everyone who believes, to the Jew first, and also to the Greek.

—Romans 1:16

But sanctify the Lord God in your hearts. Always be ready to give an answer to every man who asks you for a reason for the hope that is in you, with gentleness and fear.

—1 Peter 3:15

WORK

The LORD will open up to you His good treasure, the heavens, to give the rain to your land in its season and to bless all the work of your hand. You will lend to many nations, but you will not borrow.

—DEUTERONOMY 28:12

Let the beauty of the LORD our God be upon us, and establish the work of our hands among us; yes, establish the work of our hands.

—PSALM 90:17

Each one's work will be revealed. For the Day will declare it, because it will be revealed by fire, and the fire will test what sort of work each has done. If anyone's work which he has built on the foundation endures, he will receive a reward. If anyone's work is burned, he will suffer loss. But he himself will be saved, still going through the fire.

—1 CORINTHIANS 3:13–15

Let him who steals steal no more. Instead, let him labor, working with his hands things which are good, that he may have something to share with him who is in need.

—EPHESIANS 4:28

And whatever you do, do it heartily, as for the Lord and not for men, knowing that from the Lord you will receive the reward of the inheritance. For you serve the Lord Christ.

—Colossians 3:23–24

WORRY

The Lord also will be a refuge for the oppressed, a refuge in times of trouble. Those who know Your name will put their trust in You, for You, Lord, have not forsaken those who seek You.

—Psalm 9:9–10

God is our refuge and strength, a well-proven help in trouble. Therefore we will not fear, though the earth be removed, and though the mountains be carried into the midst of the sea; though its waters roar and foam, though the mountains shake with its swelling. Selah

—Psalm 46:1–3

The work of righteousness shall be peace, and the effect of righteousness, quietness and assurance forever.

—Isaiah 32:17

For he shall be as a tree planted by the waters, and that spreads out its roots by the river, and shall not fear when heat comes, but its leaf shall be green, and it shall not be anxious in the year of drought, neither shall cease from yielding fruit.

—Jeremiah 17:8

Be anxious for nothing, but in everything, by prayer and supplication with gratitude, make your requests known to God. And the peace of God, which surpasses all understanding, will protect your hearts and minds through Christ Jesus.

—Philippians 4:6–7

WORSHIP

I will thank the Lord according to His righteousness, and will sing praise to the name of the Lord Most High.

—Psalm 7:17

Give to the Lord the glory of His name; worship the Lord in holy splendor.

—Psalm 29:2

All the earth will worship You and will sing to You; they will sing to Your name. Selah.

—Psalm 66:4

O sing unto the Lord a new song; sing unto the Lord, all the earth!…For the Lord is great, and greatly to be praised; He is to be feared above all gods.…Honor and majesty are before Him; strength and beauty are in His sanctuary.

—Psalm 96:1–6

Give unto the Lord the glory due His name; bring an offering, and come into His courts. Worship the Lord in the beauty of holiness; tremble before Him, all the earth. Say among the nations, "The Lord reigns! Indeed, the world is established; it shall not be moved; He shall judge the peoples righteously."

—Psalm 96:8–10

Who shall not fear You, O Lord, and glorify Your name? For You alone are holy. All nations shall come and worship before You, for Your judgments have been revealed.

—Revelation 15:4

STAND STRONG ON GOD'S PROMISE

*Transform your mind, heart, and soul through
the power of God's Word, and live with joy.*

978-1-62136-566-2 | US $4.99   978-1-62136-578-5 | US $4.99   978-1-62136-610-2 | US $4.99

**MODERN
ENGLISH
VERSION**

The SpiritLed Promises series makes it easy for you
to find the perfect verse for whatever situation you face.

The MEV Bible is the most modern translation in the King James tradition.
This version accurately communicates God's Word in a way
that combines the beauty of the past with clarity for today.

12930   **AVAILABLE AT BOOKSTORES EVERYWHERE**

f ✔ Facebook.com/PassioFaith Twitter.com/PassioFaith www.PassioFaith.com

Continue Pursing a Passionate Life in the Spirit

with these FREE Newsletters

New Man
Get articles about the realities of living in today's world as a man of faith.

SpiritLed Woman
Get amazing stories, testimonies and articles on marriage, family, prayer, and more.

Charisma Magazine
Get top-trending articles, Christian teachings, entertainment reviews, videos, and more.

The Ministry Today Report
Stay informed with practical commentary, news, and articles for pastors and leaders.

Be

EMPOWERED
INSPIRED
ENCOURAGED
PASSIONATE

SIGN UP AT:
nl.charismamag.com

CHARISMA MEDIA

Enjoy your time in college, work hard, play hard. Continue to maintain good grades & maybe you can receive grants for medical school or whatever you decide to pursue! Never sell yourself short! You are brilliant and have much to offer the world. Keep writing, just journal you are extremely gifted in that area. I can see you writing books or publishing articles later in life! Work on time management you'll have less stress & great health! ♥